P9-CQZ-446

# The Proper Care of
# LABRADOR RETRIEVERS

By Dennis & Pat
Livesey

**TW-140**

*Overleaf:* Two adorable puppies from Briar Run Kennels in Warwick, NY.

The author acknowledges the contribution of Joy Quallenberg to the chapters on showing and first aid and of Chris Walkowicz to the chapters on selection, showing, and health. Additionally, the portrayal and discussion of canine pet products in this book are for instructive value only and do not necessarily constitute an endorsement by the authors, publisher, or the owners of the dogs depicted in this book.

## © 1995 by T.F.H. Publications, Inc.

Distributed in the UNITED STATES to the Pet Trade by T.F.H. Publications, Inc., One T.F.H. Plaza, Neptune City, NJ 07753; distributed in the UNITED STATES to the Bookstore and Library Trade by National Book Network, Inc. 4720 Boston Way, Lanham MD 20706; in CANADA to the Pet Trade by H & L Pet Supplies Inc., 27 Kingston Crescent, Kitchener, Ontario N2B 2T6; Rolf C. Hagen Ltd., 3225 Sartelon Street, Montreal 382 Quebec; in CANADA to the Book Trade by Vanwell Publishing Ltd., 1 Northrup Crescent, St. Catharines, Ontario L2M 6P5 ; in ENGLAND by T.F.H. Publications, PO Box 15, Waterlooville PO7 6BQ; in AUSTRALIA AND THE SOUTH PACIFIC by T.F.H. (Australia), Pty. Ltd., Box 149, Brookvale 2100 N.S.W., Australia; in NEW ZEALAND by Brooklands Aquarium Ltd. 5 McGiven Drive, New Plymouth, RD1 New Zealand; in Japan by T.F.H. Publications, Japan—Jiro Tsuda, 10-12-3 Ohjidai, Sakura, Chiba 285, Japan; in SOUTH AFRICA by Multipet Pty. Ltd., P.O. Box 35347, Northway, 4065, South Africa. Published by T.F.H. Publications, Inc.
MANUFACTURED IN THE UNITED STATES OF AMERICA
BY T.F.H. PUBLICATIONS, INC.

# Contents

# Dedication

## KELLY

YOUR LOVE FOR US WILL ALWAYS BE REMEMBERED
I MISS YOUR CLEAN LITTLE LICKS
YOUR SILLY WIGGLE
THE SMILE YOU HAD WHEN WE RUBBED YOU
YOUR SPARKLING CLEAN PUPPIES
YOUR PATIENCE AND UNCONDITIONAL LOVE
THE WAY YOU LOVED YOUR CAGE
YOU WALKING THE BULKHEAD AT THE SHORE
OUR BOAT RIDES TO THE ISLAND
THE WAY YOU WATCHED OVER THE BOYS
YOU IN THE FRONT WINDOW AT THE SHORE HOUSE
YOUR SPOT IN THE KITCHEN
YOUR PLACE NEXT TO OUR BED
THE WAY YOU RESTED YOUR HEAD ON THE BED IN THE MORNING
TO GET US UP
THE WAY YOU HERDED YOUR PUPPIES EACH DAY INTO THE BACK PEN
YOUR SILLY RUNS AROUND THE HOUSE
THE WAY YOU LOVED YOUR WALKS
YOU CARRYING OUR SOCKS
YOU CHASING YOUR TAIL
YOUR SWIMS IN THE BAY
YOUR LOVE FOR A CAR RIDE
YOUR LOVE FOR US
THANK YOU FOR ALL OF THESE GIFTS
WE LOVE YOU AND WE'LL NEVER FORGET YOU
REST IN PEACE—WE MISS YOU TERRIBLY

Snowden Hills Bets R On, better known as Kelly, ready to retrieve the ball. Owned by Amberfield Kennels.

*A chip off the old block. These two black Labs are from Amberfield Kennels. Owner, Jack Johnson, DVM.*

# The Origin of the Labrador Retriever

The history and origin of the Labrador Retriever have been researched by many experts throughout the years. Some theories and facts have surfaced that prove the Labrador's existence since 1814, referred to then as the Newfoundland Dog or the St. John's Dog. The Labrador

*The Labrador first arrived on the shores of the British Isles around the early 1800s. This is Amberfield's Darlyn owned by the authors.*

first arrived on the shores of the British Isles around the early 1800s. It was said the Labrador (meaning laborer) swam ashore from the vessels carrying cod from Newfoundland to England. He was recognized in Poole, Dorset. Mr. Charles Eley, author of the book *History of Retrievers*, describes the Labrador in this way, "It was claimed for them that their maritime existence, prolonged through countless ages, had resulted in webbed feet, a coat

Labrador Retrievers are valued by sportsmen for their fine retrieving qualities. Photo by Robert Smith.

Labradors have an inherent love of the water. This is Ch. Amberfield's Sugar Magnolia owned by Joy Quallenberg of Wustboro, NY.

impervious to water like that of an otter, and a short, thick 'swordlike' tail, with which to steer safely their stoutly made frames amid the breakers of the ocean." It is from this description that most Labrador breeders base their breeding programs and the AKC Labrador Retriever standard was derived.

We owe much to the original English

kennels from the 1940s, as it was there that many records were kept and the first Labrador clubs were established. Not everyone appreciated the unique characteristics of the Labrador; however, many of the upper-class Englishmen valued this breed's fine retrieving qualities for sportsmanship.

The color of the Labrador was assumed to be black, resembling its Newfoundland ancestors. As generations passed, however, many various traits began to appear both in color and in coat.

This is where the Flat-Coated Retriever, the chocolate Lab (also known as liver-colored), and the yellow Lab originated. Pedigrees were kept in order to help distinguish these unusual variations,

*Yellow is the most popular color for Labrador Retrievers today.*

England, sent the first Labrador Retriever to the United States as a gift. At this time the place that best suited the Labrador in the United States was Long Island. Long Island's endless shorelines and grassy fields made it a perfect place for water fowl to migrate and nest. Many sportsmen relied on the Labrador to retrieve their game unharmed. The Labrador's soft mouth and innate ability to retrieve made him an ideal choice for the hunter as both a companion and a laborer.

which were present from one generation to the next.

Lady Howe, the secretary of the first Labrador club in

As the Labrador's popularity grew and

the American Kennel Club recognized the Labrador as a separate breed of retriever, the show world became more complicated. The dual-purpose Labrador was a must during the 1930s. Field trials and shows were entered, yet for the remainder of the time Labradors were best suited for retrieving duck. For many years professional breeders started to re-evaluate their priorities among themselves and as a result the Labrador's progeny began to change. Specific

*The Labrador's loving and adaptable character make him the perfect family pet. This is Ch. Amberfield's Beach Boy pictured with the authors' sons.*

*Many sportsmen rely on the Labrador Retriever to retrieve their game unharmed. The breed's soft mouth and innate ability to retrieve make it an ideal choice as a hunting companion. Photo by Robert Smith.*

qualifications surfaced in order to produce the best type for either field purposes or the show ring.

During the 1950s the Labrador's loving and adaptable character promoted the breed in the public eye as the perfect family pet. This led to the tremendous increase in the Labrador population; some were of good quality, some were not so good. It is for this reason that breeders should take the responsibility of planning the best breedings. The history of the generations behind a dog plays a major part in the final results. Many breeders research back five generations in a line to identify specific strengths and weaknesses of the sire and dam. Fine qualities like temperament, structure, movement, and alertness have defined the Labrador as the leading retriever in field work, arson and bomb detection, Seeing Eye therapy, and family membership.

*Fine qualities like temperament, structure, movement and alertness have defined the Labrador as the leading retriever in Seeing Eye guide dogs as well as other types of assistance work.*

*Two beautiful black Labradors from Amberfield Kennels owned by Jack Johnson, DVM.*

Today the AKC takes the responsibility of recording the sire and dam of each registered dog. This allows breeders and pet owners to register their dog under a "fancier" name, using the prefix of the kennel followed by any other name. Registering your pet helps the breeders distinguish lines and also reinforces the need for all pet owners to accept the responsibilities of owning a pet.

Ch. Lobuff's Bare Necessities, bred by the Guide Dog Foundation and owned by B. Shavlik, S. Sasser, L. Agresta and E. Biegel, won Best of Breed at the 1994 Westminster Kennel Club Dog Show. Photo by Isabelle Francais.

# Standard for the Labrador Retriever

To purchase a Labrador, no less to breed a Labrador, you must know precisely what a good Labrador looks like. Every registering organization, such as the American Kennel Club or the Kennel Club of England, adopts an official standard for the breed, a description of what the ideal representative of the breed should look like.

Standards, like purebred dogs for the most part, are manmade and man-remade, which is to say they change over time. These "word pictures" are subject not only to change but also to interpretation. In a perfect world, every breeder is striving for the flawless dog, which is identical in every way to the next breeder's flawless dog, which is identical in every way to the next breeder's flawless dog. In reality, however, the flawless dog doesn't exist, never has and never will. Nonetheless, breeders strive to create that "perfect specimen" and smart owners strive to find that "perfect puppy."

Read the following breed standard carefully and repeatedly. Envision every part of the dog and ask an experienced breeder or exhibitor about anything you don't understand completely.

When buying a puppy, you should know what to look for and what NOT to look for. Pay close attention to disqualifications and faults. When considering gait, remember that your puppy is but a "toddler"; instead observe the movement of the parents or other relatives. Structure as well as movement are

passed along from parent to offspring.

**General Appearance**—The Labrador Retriever is a strongly built, medium-sized, short-coupled

*When considering gait, remember that your puppy is still a toddler. Movement as well as structure are passed along from parent to offspring. This is Breezy of Breezy Labradors.*

dog possessing a sound, athletic, well-balanced conformation that enables it to function as a retrieving gun dog; the substance and soundness to hunt waterfowl or upland game for long hours under difficult conditions; the character and quality to win in the show ring; and the temperament to be a family companion. Physical features and mental characteristics should denote a dog bred to perform as an efficient retriever of game with a stable temperament suitable for a variety of pursuits beyond the hunting environment.

The most distinguishing

*A beautiful head on a Briar Run Labrador.*

characteristics of the Labrador Retriever are its short, dense, weather-resistant coat; an "otter" tail; a clean-cut head with broad back skull and moderate stop; powerful jaws; and its "kind," friendly eyes, expressing character, intelligence and good temperament.

Above all, a Labrador Retriever must be well balanced, enabling it to move in the show ring or work in the field with little or no effort. The typical Labrador possesses style and quality without over refinement, and substance without lumber or cloddiness. The Labrador is bred primarily as a working gun dog; structure and soundness are of great importance.

**Size, Proportion and Substance—** *Size*—The height at the withers for a dog is $22\frac{1}{2}$ to $24\frac{1}{2}$ inches; for a bitch is $21\frac{1}{2}$ to $23\frac{1}{2}$ inches. Any variance greater than $\frac{1}{2}$ inch above or below these heights is a disqualification. Approximate weight of

*Your Labrador can grow to be from 55 to 80 pounds. At 14 weeks of age, Amberfield's Bo Regard has a lot more growing to do. Owners, Marci and Dave O'Brien.*

dogs and bitches in working condition: dogs 65 to 80 pounds; bitches 55 to 70 pounds.

The minimum height ranges set forth in the paragraph above shall not apply to dogs or bitches under twelve months of age.

*Proportion*—Short-coupled: length from the point of the shoulder to the point of the rump is equal to or slightly longer than the distance from the withers to the ground. Distance from the elbow to the ground should be equal to one half of the height at the withers. The brisket should extend to the elbows, but not perceptibly deeper. The body must be of

*Labrador Retrievers should be shown in working condition, well-muscled and without excess fat. This is Amberfield's Wetlands Woodie, a son of Ch. Amberfield's Beach Boy. Owners, Skip and Anne Storer.*

*Substance*— Substance and bone proportionate to the overall dog. Light, "weedy" individuals are definitely incorrect; equally objectionable are cloddy lumbering specimens. Labrador Retrievers shall be shown in working condition, well-muscled and without excess fat.

**Head**—*Skull*–the skull should be wide; well developed but without exaggeration. The skull and foreface should be on parallel planes and of approximately equal length. There should be a moderate stop—the brow slightly pronounced so that the skull is not absolutely in a straight line with the nose. The brow sufficient length to permit a straight, free and efficient stride; but the dog should never appear low and long or tall and leggy in outline.

*The Labrador's head should be clean cut and free from fleshy cheeks; the bony structure of the skull is chiseled beneath the eye with no prominence in the cheek. This is Saltwater's Hot Rescue Ranger.*

ridges aid in defining the stop. The head should be clean-cut and free from fleshy cheeks; the bony structure of the skull chiseled beneath the eye with no prominence in the cheek. The skull may show some median line; the occipital bone

*The nose of the Labrador Retriever should be wide and the nostrils well developed. The nose should be brown on chocolate Labs. Photo by Robert Smith.*

is not conspicuous in mature dogs. Lips should not be squared off or pendulous, but fall away in a curve toward the throat. A wedge-shape head, or a head long and narrow in muzzle and back skull, is incorrect as are massive, cheeky heads. The jaws are powerful and free from snippiness–the muzzle neither long and narrow nor short and stubby. *Nose*—The nose should be wide and the nostrils well-developed. The nose should be black on black or yellow dogs, and brown on chocolates. Nose color fading to a lighter shade is not a fault. A thoroughly pink nose or one lacking in any pigment is a disqualification. *Teeth*—The teeth should be strong and regular with a scissors bite; the lower teeth just behind, but touching the inner side of the upper incisors. A level bite is acceptable, but not desirable. Undershot, overshot or misaligned teeth are serious faults. Full dentition is preferred. Missing molars or pre-molars are serious faults. *Ears*—The ears should hang moderately close to the head, set rather far back, and somewhat low on the skull; slightly above eye level. Ears should not be large and heavy, but in proportion with the skull and reach to the inside of the eye when pulled forward. *Eyes*—Kind, friendly eyes imparting good temperament, intelligence and alertness are a hallmark of the breed. They should be of medium size, set well apart, and neither protruding nor deep set. Eye color should be brown in black and yellow Labradors, and brown or hazel in chocolates. Black or yellow eyes give a harsh expression and are undesirable. Small eyes set close together or round prominent eyes are not typical of the breed. Eye rims are black in black and yellow Labradors; and

*The Labrador's eyes are kind and friendly. Intelligence and alertness are a hallmark of the breed. Owner, Denise Evans. Photo by Isabelle Francais.*

brown in chocolates. Eye rims without pigmentation is a disqualification.

**Neck, Topline and Body**—*Neck*—The neck should be of proper length to allow the dog to retrieve game easily. It should be muscular and free from throatiness. The neck should rise strongly from the shoulders with a moderate arch. A short, thick neck or a "ewe" neck is incorrect. *Topline*—The back is strong and the topline is level from the withers to the croup when standing or moving. However, the loin should show evidence of flexibility for athletic endeavor. *Body*—The Labrador should be short-

*The neck of the Labrador Retriever should be of proper length to allow the dog to retrieve game easily. Photo by Robert Smith.*

*The back of the Labrador Retriever is strong and the topline is level from the withers to the croup when standing or moving.*

coupled, with good spring of ribs tapering to a moderately wide chest. The Labrador should not be narrow chested, giving the appearance of hollowness between the front legs, nor should it have a wide spreading, bulldog-like front. Correct chest conformation will result in tapering between the front legs that allows unrestricted forelimb movement. Chest breadth that is either too wide or too narrow

*When viewed from the side, the Lab shows a well-developed, but not exaggerated, forechest.*

almost straight, with little or no tuck-up in mature animals. Loins should be short, wide and strong; extending to well-developed powerful hindquarters. When viewed from the side, the Labrador Retriever shows a well-developed, but not exaggerated, forechest. *Tail*—The tail is a distinguishing feature of the breed. It should be very thick at the base, gradually tapering toward the tip, of medium length, and extending no longer than to the hock. The tail should be free from feathering and clothed thickly all around with the Labrador's short, dense coat, thus having that peculiar

for efficient movement and stamina is incorrect. Slab-sided individuals are not typical of the breed; equally objectionable are rotund or barrel chested specimens. The underline is rounded appearance that has been described as the "otter" tail. The tail should follow the topline in repose or when in motion. It may be carried gaily, but should not curl over the back. Extremely short tails or long thin tails are serious faults. The tail completes the balance of the Labrador by giving it a flowing line from the top of the head to the tip of the tail. Docking

*The Labrador should be short-coupled, with good spring of ribs tapering to a moderately wide chest.*

or otherwise altering the length or natural carriage of the tail is a disqualification.

**Forequarters—** Forequarters should be muscular, well coordinated and balanced with the hindquarters. *Shoulders*—The shoulders are well laid-back, long and sloping, forming an angle with the upper arm of approximately 90 degrees that permits the dog to move his forelegs in an easy manner with strong forward reach. Ideally, the length of the shoulder blade should equal the length of the upper arm. Straight shoulder blades, short upper arms or heavily muscled or loaded shoulders, all restricting free movement, are

*The "otter" tail completes the balance of the Labrador by giving him a flowing line from the top of the head to the tip of the tail. This is Amberfield's Darlyn.*

incorrect. *Front Legs*—When viewed from the front, the legs should be straight with good strong bone. Too much bone is as undesirable as too little bone, and short legged, heavy boned individuals are not typical of the breed. Viewed from the side, the elbows should be directly under the withers, and the front legs should be perpendicular to the ground and well under the body. The elbows should be close to the ribs without looseness. Tied-in elbows or being "out at the elbows" interfere with free movement and are serious faults. Pasterns should be strong and short and should slope slightly from the perpendicular line of the leg. Feet are strong and compact, with well-arched toes and well-developed pads. Dew claws may be removed. Splayed feet, hare feet, knuckling over, or feet turning in or out are serious faults.

**Hindquarters**—The Labrador's hindquarters are broad, muscular and well-developed from the hip to the hock with well-turned stifles and strong short hocks. Viewed from the rear, the hind legs are straight and parallel. Viewed from the side, the angulation of the rear legs is in balance with the front. The hind legs are strongly boned, muscled with moderate angulation at the stifle, and powerful, clearly defined thighs. The stifle is strong and there is no slippage of the patella while in motion or when standing. The hock joints are strong, well let down and do not slip or hyper-extend while in motion or when standing. Angulation of both stifle and hock joint is such as to achieve the optimal balance of drive and traction. When standing the rear toes are only slightly behind the point of the rump. Over-angulation produces a sloping topline not typical of the breed. Feet are strong and compact, with well-arched toes hocks and over-angulation are serious structural defects and are to be faulted.

**Coat**—The coat is a

*Chocolate Labs can vary in shade from light to dark chocolate. Owner, Denise Evans. Photo by Isabelle Francais.*

and well-developed pads. Cow-hocks, spread hocks, sickle distinctive feature of the Labrador Retriever. It should be short, straight and very dense, giving a fairly hard feeling to the hand. The Labrador should have a soft, weather-resistant undercoat that provides protection from water, cold and all types of ground cover. A slight wave down the back is permissible. Woolly coats, soft silky coats, and sparse slick coats are not typical of the breed, and should be severely penalized.

**Color**—The Labrador Retriever coat colors are black, yellow and chocolate. Any other color or a combination of colors is a disqualification. A small white spot on the chest is permissible, but not desirable.

White hairs from aging or scarring are not to be misinterpreted as brindling. *Black*— Blacks are all black. A black with brindle markings or a black with tan markings is a disqualification. *Yellow*—Yellows may range in color from fox-red to light cream, with variations in shading on the ears, back and underparts of the dog. *Chocolate*—Chocolates can vary in shade from light to dark chocolate. Chocolate with brindle or tan markings is a disqualification.

**Movement**— Movement of the Labrador Retriever should be free and effortless. When watching a dog move

*A yellow Lab and a black Lab owned by Lisa Beaurais. Photo by Isabelle Francais.*

toward oneself, there should be no sign of elbows out. Rather, the elbows should be held neatly to the body with the legs not too close together. Moving straight forward without pacing or weaving, the legs should form straight lines, with all

*The authors' sons with their Christmas puppy from Amberfield Kennels.*

parts moving in the same plane. Upon viewing the dog from the rear, one should have the impression that the hind legs move as nearly as possible in a parallel line with the front legs. The hocks should do their full share of the work, flexing well, giving the appearance of power and strength, When viewed from the side, the shoulders should move freely and effortlessly, and the foreleg should reach forward close to the ground with extension. A short, choppy movement or high knee action indicates a straight shoulder; paddling indicates long, weak pasterns: and a short, stilted rear gait indicates a straight rear assembly; all are serious faults. Movement faults interfering with performance, including weaving; side-winding; crossing over; high knee action; paddling; and

*The Labrador's gentle ways make him an ideal family dog. Owners, Jen and Al Wolyniec.*

short, choppy movement should be severely penalized.

**Temperament—** True Labrador Retriever temperament is as much a hallmark of the breed as the "otter" tail. The ideal disposition is one of a kindly, outgoing, tractable nature; eager to please and non-aggressive towards man or animal. The Labrador has much that appeals to people: his gentle ways, intelligence and adaptability make him an ideal dog. Aggressiveness toward humans or other animals, or any evidence of shyness in an adult, should be severely penalized.

*DISQUALIFICATIONS*

1. Any deviation from the height prescribed in the Standard.

2. A thoroughly pink nose or one lacking in any pigment.

3. Eye rims without pigment.

4. Docking or otherwise altering the length or natural carriage of the tail.

5. Any other color or a combination of colors other than black, yellow or chocolate as described in the Standard.

Approval Date: February 12, 1994

Effective Date: March 31, 1994

©The American Kennel Club, Inc., 1994

*The ideal disposition of a Labrador Retriever is one of a kindly, outgoing, tractable nature. Agent, Stephen Wojculewski. Photo by Isabelle Francais.*

*Drew Livesey and Donna, a yellow Labrador owned by Gene and Sally Mitchell.*

# The Right Owner for a Lab

Is a Labrador Retriever a good family dog? How is he with children? What happens when we leave him alone during the day? These are some of the many questions we ask ourselves when we think about acquiring a dog. The real answers to these questions are not that simple because it's the individual owner who must match his personality with that of the breed he is considering.

The Labrador owner is a person who possesses the need to share physical affection, for a Lab seeks attention from his owner. Labs love to be endlessly stroked and scratched—many will even collapse at your feet and roll onto their backs, anticipating the joy of your touch. They remind us of teddy bears, lying there with their paws in the air, silly smiles on their faces, and a satisfied expression in their soft eyes. It's times like these that will grip your heart, even when your Lab is long gone, because this memory

*The ideal Labrador owner is affectionate and outgoing with his dog. This is Dr. Martin Sturman with Ambleside Amelia owned by Dr. and Mrs. Henry Kissenger and Ambleside Wheel Watcher owned by Julie Sturman and Connie Demorest.*

of warmth and love will always be with you.

Don't expect to make a move without your Lab at your feet eager to obey your next command. As I sit here, my three Labradors are lying at my feet. They appear to be resting comfortably; however, my slightest move or even a shift in eye contact is enough to start them thump-thump-thumping their tails and hoping I'll call them over for one more petting session.

"People on the go" seems to describe most of us. If you are this type of person, keep in mind that Labradors are ready before you are. Labrador people enjoy sharing mundane errands with their Lab propped up on the seat next to them or riding side-saddle in the back of their four-wheeler. Labs share the same enthusiasm as you when going on vacation to the shore, lake, woods, and mountains.

*Labradors are affectionate towards children. This is Ch. Killingworth Bonny of Dimeno, CD, CGC with Brooke Huttner. Bonny is owned by Julie Sturman.*

Labradors, like children, remember the wonderful trips you take together and whine as they approach their favorite spot in anticipation of the freedom and companionship that is so important in their lives, as it is in our own.

Labradors don't mind the rain and therefore you only need to invest in one set of rain gear—for yourself. The sun doesn't have to shine in order for your Labrador to be ready for a hike in the woods or a walk around the lake—any weather will do. One of the funniest things to watch is your pup's first encounter with snow. They are

inquisitive little creatures and the fluffy white stuff is enticing. They prance through the snow like deer, leaping in it, bouncing in it, and burying their noses in it. A hunter's

*Children should be able to share in the responsibilities of dog ownership. These two Labs are enjoying a walk with their young owners, Wesley and Troy Livesey.*

quest is more in reach with a Labrador at his side. The thrill of the search is innately part of the Labrador's nature. As a sporting dog, he is rugged, reliable, and always ready for adventure.

Adaptable to almost any environment, Labradors can fit any lifestyle, whether you live in a city, small town, or rural area. Size doesn't inhibit a Lab from living in an apartment, as long as he gets his daily exercise. Keep in mind that your Lab will mold himself after your personality. They respond to your immediate emotions. Therefore, your temperament and reactions to routine situations will reinforce the positive or negative responses of your dog. You must be willing to accommodate your dog's needs without warning or resentment as they arise.

Labradors are like children, they feel needed when they are expected to follow the rules of the household. Children and Labs view their parents/owners as people who offer them love and affection if they are good and do the right things. Positive attention enhances the growth of your Lab's spirit which will last his whole life.

The Labrador Retriever possesses many superior qualities that are unique to the breed.

*Labradors are adaptable to almost any environment as long as they can get their daily exercise. Photo by Karen Taylor.*

*Labs are gentle and instinctively protective towards infants. This is Agber's Darlyn inspecting the newest member of the family.*

Labradors are affectionate towards infants and children. It may be difficult for the non-dog lover to believe that our six-year-old female yellow Lab instinctively protected my sleeping infant son from a passerby who wanted to peek in at him. Labs are faithful to their owners. Although when left alone he may act the part of the contented pet, your Lab constantly longs for your company. The female Labrador Retriever is one of the few who finds motherhood a pleasure and cleans her pups until their fur sparkles. This, however, is not to say motherhood is for every female Lab and breeding should be left up to the established, educated breeder. Above all the Labrador Retriever is an intelligent and perceptive pet. When a family introduces a new infant into the family, most siblings are cautioned on how to handle the new baby. It has been my experience that our Labrador was the only family member instinctively aware of the delicate nature of our newborn son. A Lab's soft nature guides him through these tender moments. The Labrador's easygoing disposition allows you to correct his mistakes properly before bad habits develop. Most breeders suggest that a crate be used during training so that your pet won't be given the opportunity to destroy your home. Following a daily schedule will usually be enough to train and housebreak your Lab.

It is important that the owner be in tune with his dog's need to be useful. A Lab is always willing to please his owner. The Labrador was bred to retrieve fishing nets in the icy waters of Newfoundland. Labradors thrive on carrying sticks, balls,

*Labs are ready to accompany their owners on any adventure. These eager pups are owned by Gene and Sally Mitchell.*

and even your newspaper just to show you their dedication. This loyal and understanding breed must be appreciated for their diverse abilities as companions and retrievers. Therefore, the right owner should be aware of the Labrador's sensitive disposition. This is why it's essential that you spend time each day either exercising or training your Lab to retrieve. His reward is your attention and companionship, which will foster an eternal bond between you and your pet.

*Chunky pup from a litter bred by Mary Baker, Woodland Kennels, Bellport, NY.*

# Selecting Your Labrador Retriever

## PICKING THE RIGHT PUPPY

Buying a puppy should not be an impulsive endeavor; it is never wise to rush out and buy just any puppy that catches your shopping eye. The more time and thought you invest, the greater your satisfaction with your new companion. And if this new companion is to be purely a pet, its background and early care will affect its future health and good temperament. It is always essential that you choose a properly raised puppy from healthy, well-bred stock.

You must seek out an active, sturdy puppy with bright eyes and an intelligent expression. If the puppy is friendly, that's a major plus, but you don't want one that is hyperactive nor do you want one that is dull and listless. The coat should be clean and plush, with no signs of fleas or other parasites. The premises should be clean, by sight and smell, and the proprietors should be helpful and knowledgeable. A reputable seller wants his customers satisfied and will therefore represent the puppy fairly. Let good common sense guide your purchase, and choose a **reliable,** well-recommended source that you know has well-satisfied customers. Don't look for a bargain, since you may end up paying many times over in future veterinarian bills, not to mention disappointment and heartache if your pet turns out not to be well.

*Choosing a pup from this adorable litter of yellow Labs will not be easy. A lot of time and thought should be invested before you make a final decision.*

## SELECTING A PUPPY TO SHOW

A puppy might grow up to be a good pet. Or he can be much more

and enhanced by the knowledgeable selection of this future Super Dog.

Choosing to share our lives with a dog is only the first step of a decision-filled time. We must determine also which breed best suits us and our lifestyle. It's wise to be prepared for several questions that will arise: Male or female? Adult or puppy? Did we select this breed for its special qualities and abilities or simply because we like its appearance or temperament?

Within a breed—even within a litter—personality differences are found, and buyers should specify whether they want the one who

than that: a blue-ribbon winner, a helpmate, a marvel of ability and, certainly, a beloved companion. The pup's future possibilities are restricted only by the owner's goals for him

*Seek out an active, sturdy puppy with bright eyes and an intelligent expression. Photo by Isabelle Francais.*

whether competition in obedience or achieving a championship is a priority.

**MAKING CONNECTIONS**

When a serious fancier chooses a dog to fulfill hopes and dreams, more is involved than simply finding a litter of the chosen breed and picking the pup with the waggiest tail or the lickingest tongue. First, a breeder with an impeccable reputation must be found. For those who are already involved in the dog world, it's less difficult to make connections because they are aware of preferences in structure or in ability and have an idea as to

bounces off the walls or the one who sleeps 23 hours a day. Other preferences, such as size or color, might be stated. A potential exhibitor should say which lines produce well in these respects.

The recent enthusiast may have to overcome a few more obstacles, but the goal is worth the trouble. When people want the best, they haunt the places where the best are found. When Cape Cod tourists crave a fresh clam bake, they go to the beach, not the all-night grocery. The finest wines are found at first-class restaurants, not at a lunch counter. And the same is true of dogs. According to various interests, the superior

*Although these two black Labs seem identical, each one has his own personality and tastes. Your breeder will be able to tell you much about the puppy you choose. Photo by Isabelle Francais.*

The pup you choose should have a clean, plush coat with no signs of fleas or other parasites. Owner, Frank Purdy. Photo by Isabelle Francais.

dogs will be at shows, trials or tests.

While studying the dogs who are esthetically pleasing and who perform in the manner admired, make notes on the kennels that boast the winners. Which sires and dams produce consistently? Their owners are the blue-ribbon breeders. Even if these kennels do not have puppies available, they are the places to start. Most owners are willing and able to recommend other breeders, and these people usually refer you only to places that they would buy from themselves. Giving a poor reference reflects on their own reputation; therefore, they stick to those with a four-star rating.

Starting at the root with a quality breeder allows a buyer to branch off if necessary. Show kennels have a monetary as well as an emotional investment at stake and seek excellence in the

*If possible, try to see the parents of the pup you choose. Temperament as well as type are passed on from parent to offspring. Photo by Isabelle Francais.*

*Make notes on kennels that boast the winners. This is Ch. Polywog Comic of Chidley owned by Dennis Livesey.*

handlers, groomers and veterinarians with whom they do business. These professionals are additional sources of referrals. They often know who has litters, as well as who has top-notch animals and a squeaky clean reputation. Handlers, vets and groomers have a stake in the matter, too, because they might gain a client from someone who follows their lead and is pleased.

Dog clubs can supply reliable contacts as well. Many have a breeder index or answering services for just this purpose. The American Kennel Club can furnish the secretaries' names of sanctioned all-breed and specialty clubs, both locally and nationally. Often clubs are listed with the Chamber of

*A dog show is a good place to view superior Labs as well as a good start for finding the perfect Lab for you. These littermates are Ch. Amberfield's Beach Boy and Sugar Magnolia.*

*Champions beget champions. This is Summer Sun II, the sire of Amberfield's Beach Boy. Owner, Ken Golden.*

Commerce or in the telephone book. The Kennel Club of Great Britain is the appropriate source for British residents, as is the Canadian Kennel Club.

Some clubs have a code of ethics which the breeders must sign and adhere to in order to be recommended. Money-minded profiteers are seldom found within the ranks of clubs because they have no interest in supporting and working at shows, seminars or canine charity fundraisers.

Ads in canine magazines and newspapers are costly, and kennels who advertise are usually secure, well-established businesses with owners who have a reputation to maintain. It is up to us to determine just how fine that reputation is. "Brag" ads trumpeting the kennel's latest Field Trial Champion or Best in Show Winner can give clues of success within a specific field of interest.

*The search for the perfect puppy is one that requires equal parts of emotion and logic, and not something that should be rushed into or taken lightly. Owner, Jeannine Biddle. Photo by Isabelle Francais.*

Published breed books, such as this one, display photos of top-winning dogs and descriptions of the kennels that produced them. The motto, "Records live, opinions die" is a truism. Any kennel that claims winners numbering in the double digits or above has begun its own records.

Of course, the professional breeder who is just starting up the ladder offers advantages as well. Because he doesn't have the widespread reputation, he is less likely to have waiting lists. Frequently, the person from whom he bought his bitch or who owns the stud he used will refer inquiries to him.

Although cost should not be number one on our list when searching for a companion, it is a consideration for most of us, and a beginner seldom can demand the prices of the established breeder. If the dedicated

*A puppy may grow up to be a blue-ribbon winner. Owner, Denise Evans. Photo by Isabelle Francais.*

newcomer has bought his foundation stock from a reputable kennel, very likely he will have animals for sale that are comparable in quality to his mentor's. Not everyone who looks for a new, snazzy car can afford to buy a Mercedes. Some of us have to be satisfied with a well-built Chevrolet. And that Chevy can be attractive and dependable too. We don't always have to buy top-of-the-line to obtain quality, as long as we stay away from the junkyard.

*The authors' pride and joy, Amberfield's Beach Boy, as a puppy.*

### NETWORKING

In conducting any type of research, one lead suggests another. A contact list mushrooms and grows, giving the buyer several options.

When contacting a well-known kennel and finding no puppies available, it is helpful to ask, "Can you recommend someone?" Or, "I just

*A litter of yellow Labs from England. Photo by Robert Smith.*

love your stud, Alf (or your bitch, Tigger). Does anyone have puppies with those lines?" Who can resist a compliment like that?

Ask breeders whether they belong to a local club and the national breed club.

Club membership shows a sustained interest in the breed and in dogs.

### SEARCHING FOR SUPER DOG

Finding the ideal dog is not a whit easier than looking for the ideal mate. Of course, it's a bit less complicated to rid ourselves of an unwanted beast if it's the four-legged kind, but failure is not the object of conducting this search. It's finding a buddy, a companion, one who appeals to us in every sense and will still do so when he's old, gray and pot-bellied.

When it comes to welcoming a new member into a family, spending the time to find the right addition is well worth the effort. It can't be done by placing an ad in the personal want ad section: Tall, athletic man of 40 desires a jogging companion who is cute, fuzzy and has floppy ears.

*At dog shows you can look at several examples of the breed which will help you to choose your Labrador puppy. This is Amberfield's Wetlands Woodie.*

How then? Buyers should look at several examples of the breed before plunging into a ten-to-fifteen-year commitment. Many who have experience and have developed an "eye" know immediately whether or not a particular litter is going to offer promise. But those who are buying a dog

A yellow Lab puppy from Amberfield Kennels awakes to greet his potential owners.

*Yellow Labrador photographed by Robert Smith.*

for the first time or who are engaged in an initial search for this particular breed need to see more than one specimen to make such a decision. And it's best not to base a choice on a picture in a book or a television commercial, unless you've had the opportunity to see the dog in reality and in action.

Certain questions arise that can only be answered through a one-on-one session. Can I live with the energy of this breed/individual? Is this dog too aloof for me?

*Observe how the puppies interact with their littermates. You want to choose the one that is neither too shy nor too aggressive. Owner, Amberfield Kennels.*

Even if the dog of our dreams lives 2,000 miles away and it's impossible to make a speculative jaunt, buyers can observe the breed at shows or by hunting down a specimen that lives within 200 miles. Two hundred miles is too far? How far should you travel to find someone who is going to inhabit a corner of your life, your home and your heart for the next dozen years?

When the selection is narrowed down to one or two breeders and litters, and it comes to making a choice of the individual, this can be done even if the 2,000-mile trek isn't feasible. Of course, we have already ascertained that the breeder is reputable, so relying on his expertise and experience with the lines is helpful. Matchmaking is his business. He has everything to gain by ensuring the happiness of the new owner (and thereby the pup's) and everything to lose if it turns out to be a match made in hell.

Photos are a necessity in making a long-distance selection. Some modern-technology breeders offer videos to prospective buyers, demonstrating each puppy's movement, structure, attitude and interaction with littermates. A few think to film the sire during the nuptial visit and the dam prior to the loss of her willowy figure.

*This yellow puppy will surely impress his new owners with his clean teeth and fresh breath after chewing on his Plaque Attacker Dental Bone™ from Nylabone.® Photo by Isabelle Francais.*

Professional handlers can assist in the search in return for a finder's fee and the promise of a new client. If the pro appears at the door with a scraggly hag instead of the voluptuous vamp of our dreams, it's no go and no dough.

## ONE ON ONE

If we're fortunate enough to live in the same vicinity as the kennel, we can conduct our own evaluation and perhaps participate in a temperament or aptitude test of the litter. Certain other subtleties can be assessed as well, such as the breeder's rapport with his dogs. An unspoken but obvious bond should be present, passing from one to the other. . . a look of devotion when the dam looks at her owner. . . pride shining on the face of the breeder and soft affection for the dogs in his eyes. . . an almost automatic caress of a velvet ear during the buyer's interview. . . a wet nose nuzzling under an arm.

Happy, healthy dogs greet visitors at the door. Firm but gentle corrections are given and obeyed—at least partially, during the excitement of having guests. Needless to say, the sire and dam must be sound in mind and body as well as typical of the breed—

*Bring the whole family along when making the final decision so that all may have a hand in choosing the new family member. Owner Andrew Livesey has made his choice!*

that is, they look like Beagles instead of Bassets or vice versa. Although the sire is seldom a roommate of the dam, the breeder should have photos and a pedigree of the dog available for viewing.

Buyers should be prepared to ask questions as well as to answer them. Does the breeder belong to a club, has he ever shown, and do any of his dogs have titles? Does he linebreed, inbreed or outcross? Negative answers do not necessarily mean "Buyer Beware." The breeder should have answers, however, to educated questions and not say, "Huh?" or "Got no time for such foolishness."

It is our duty to discover whether any problems exist in our breed and whether the breeder has taken steps to avoid them. For instance, are his breeding animals OFA1 certified for good hips and CERF1 cleared for normal eyes? VWD1, OCD1, hypothyroidism, deafness and epilepsy, in addition to other conditions, are hereditary and should not be present in breeding stock. If we're interested in becoming breeders ourselves, a free-whelping line and superlative foundation stock are pluses.

When appropriate, ask about and examine for entropion,

earsets, incorrect bites and missing teeth, as well as other problems that may be known to appear in the breed. If we've done our homework, mismarks and improper coats should be apparent, but one should be aware of less obvious breed faults also.

## MAKING THE GRADE

Those who wish to conduct formal temperament tests should do so when the puppies are seven weeks of age. These tests not only help breeders and buyers determine which pups are over-aggressive or horribly shy (hopefully none), but they show

*After studying the winning Labradors, you should have a good idea of what you are looking for in your new puppy. This is Ch. Amberfield's Sugar Magnolia shown by Lisa Weiss Agresta.*

the range of good temperaments and obedience aptitude.

Pups should be tested separately, preferably on new turf by someone unknown to them. When the tester or surroundings is familiar, tendencies may be hidden or exaggerated.

In each instance, note whether the pups are bold, shy or curious. If a pup startles or is hesitant, does he recover and respond to the tester positively?

*An impressive litter from Amberfield Kennels.*

**Social tests:**

1. Observe the pup's reaction to the strange place and to a stranger. Is he bold, shy or curious? Note whether he bounces around immediately confident, hides in a corner or takes a moment to gain his composure and then begins to explore.

2. The tester should bend or kneel and call the puppy to him in a friendly manner, clapping or whistling if he wishes.

3. The tester stands and walks away, calling to the pup.

**Dominance tests:**

4. Rolling the pup on his back, the tester holds him in place for 30 seconds.

5. A stranger pets the pup on his head and looks directly at him, putting his face close to the pup's.

6. Pick up the pup with hands under the belly; hold elevated for 30 seconds.

**Alertness/ obedience tests:**

7. Crumple noisy paper or rattle a stone inside a can.

8. Toss the paper or a toy to see if the pup retrieves and returns the object.

9. Drag a towel or similar object in front of the pup. Does he show curiosity and follow?

**Responses:**

The bold, naughty or aggressive pup reacts immediately, sometimes barking or biting. This pup struggles during the restraint or dominance tests. He might grab at the tester's clothing. A top dog such as this one needs a dominant owner, a person who is willing—and able—to train, discipline and maintain control.

At the other end of the scale is the pup who shrinks away, shows disinterest or hides. He might cry or give in immediately during the restraint and dominance tests. The underdog takes a patient owner, one who is willing to encourage and socialize.

In between is the pup who is friendly, accepting and rather middle of the road. He might be hesitant, but is cooperative in most efforts. This one should fit in almost any home!

The ideal obedience prospect would willingly follow and come. He'd also be alert and show curiosity; he'd run after the toy, pick it up and return it to the tester.

*To test a puppy's alertness and obedience, toss a toy and see if the puppy retrieves it. The ideal prospect would be alert and curious. Owner, Amberfield Kennels.*

## NARROWING IT DOWN

Breeders have the additional advantage of living with the litter for eight or more weeks. They are the best ones to know which pup is the pack leader, which one follows docilely and which one tries to topple the king of the mountain off his perch. Notes should be made on eager or picky eaters. Individual descriptions using such adjectives as rowdy or laid-back, outgoing or aloof, and independent or willing to please are helpful during matchmaking.

When initial contact is made with the seller, we should specify what type of personality is desired

*Pick me! Pick me! Puppies bred at The Seeing Eye in NJ.*

in our future pet. A "type A" perfectionist or workaholic will find it difficult to live with a rough-and-tumble, devil-take-care livewire who is trying out for the next *Rambo* sequel. Nor would the 78-year-old gent who likes to snooze by the evening fire want to go home with the canine yo-yo. (But this pup would be perfect for the athletic man wanting a jogging companion in that personal ad.)

The one absolute no-no is picking a dog because you feel sorry for him. Sorry lasts a long time. Rarely does a new home cure timidity, illness or anti-social behavior.

An owner who intends to field trial or hunt with his dog wants to find one who has a good nose and high energy. Dangle a bird feather on a rod and see whether the pup reacts by flash or sight pointing. Marked timidity shown during household pan rattling or door slamming wouldn't fare well for a dog who's expected to join in the hunt. A bold,

*A good time to pick your Labrador puppy is anywhere from eight to ten weeks of age. By this time they should have learned canine socialization from their dam and littermates. Owner, Amberfield Kennels.*

independent dog who shows curiosity is desirable.

want, it might be necessary to make a reservation long before our future dream pup sets a paw on the ground. After all, if we admire what is trotting out of this kennel's gates, we should realize a few others might have recognized its quality as well. Breeders who consistently produce well often have long waiting lists.

Before selecting a kennel to honor with the purchase, other factors can be discussed with the seller in advance. Be aware of the guarantee offered, what the contract covers and whether this kennel has established a reputation for standing

## BUYING A PIECE OF THE FUTURE

Some buyers place a deposit for a puppy sight unseen, sometimes even before the litter is born or bred! When we find a breeder who is producing the style, type and movement we behind its dogs.

Certain minimal records should accompany every pup: a pedigree, a registration blank, medical records, feeding and grooming instructions, a sales contract and some type of guarantee.

Registration papers are a necessity for the serious fancier who wishes to show and breed. ILP (Individual Listing Privilege) may be shown in obedience as can Limited Registration dogs who may also participate in a few instinct tests. They may not, however, be exhibited in the conformation ring. The American Kennel Club requires ILP dogs (other than those in the Miscellaneous Classes) to be spayed or neutered, and the Limited Registration stamp, begun in 1990, prevents the limited dog's progeny from being registered. These steps were taken by the AKC to discourage indiscriminate breeding practices.

A pedigree should contain at least three generations, with four to six being preferable. Pedigrees tell us more than the names and titles of ancestors. The knowledgeable person can tell whether a pup is linebred, outcrossed or inbred, as well as health certifications such as OFA. CERF numbers are also often included, as are colors.

*A pedigree strong in obedience titles should give an indication that the puppy's family demonstrates trainability and intelligence both in the field and at home. Owners, Kathy and Ted McCue. Photo by Isabelle Francais.*

A pedigree strong in obedience titles should give an indication that the pup's family demonstrates trainability and intelligence. Likewise, several championship titles are encouraging. Quality begets quality.

An eight-week-old pup should not have a lengthy medical record, but this paper should note a physical exam and at least one combination inoculation. If the litter has been wormed, this should also be noted.

A good age to pick a puppy is when the

*Lines vary within a country as well as from country to country. British Labradors used for shooting are more athletic in their type and appearance. Photo by Robert Smith.*

litter is from eight to ten weeks old. By this time, they have learned canine socialization skills from their dam and littermates. With plenty of TLC given by the breeder as a background, sound puppies easily transfer their affection to a new family.

Lines and breeds vary, but many knowledgeable breeders prefer to pick their show prospects between eight to twelve weeks of age. Follow the breeder's advice; nobody knows the lines better than he does.

Occasionally the subject of co-ownership arises. This may create the best of times or the worst of times; it certainly forges the members of a paper relationship into the best of friends or festers them into the worst of enemies. An offer of co-ownership does signify that the breeder has faith in the dog. After all, he wouldn't want to co-own a poor specimen.

A decision can be made depending upon the strings of the co-ownership and whether the two parties can work together. Simple co-ownership

agreements may require one puppy back from a breeding or stud rights. More complicated contracts demand half a litter—or half of every

*Little by little this puppy's eyes are opening at ten days of age. Owner, Andrew Livesey.*

litter, exhibition requirements, the hiring of an expensive professional handler, or more. If breeder and buyer are congenial and willing to bend when situations not covered in the contract arise, a co-ownership can be an opportunity to purchase a dog or bitch normally beyond our price range.

## BENEFITS OF OWNERSHIP

The benefits of owning a pet are many, among them pride, social, educational, acceptance, and responsibility. We are often proud of owning a

*These three Labs from England are enjoying some time in the water. Photo by Robert Smith.*

*Pets teach children responsibility. This young owner is practicing preventive dental care by giving her Lab a Nylabone®. Photo by Karen Taylor.*

beautiful animal (remembering that beauty is in the eye of the beholder) whose coat shines with health and whose eyes sparkle with glee at our approach. We can make friends and establish relationships through our dog. Kids and adults both learn responsibility through caring for the pet. We educate ourselves to provide physical care and, if we so desire, the intricacies of the dog world—as far as we want to go. Our dog doesn't care at what stage we stop learning. Acceptance comes because our dog always greets us with affection, no matter what our age, race, creed, size or abilities.

But probably the most important benefit is psychological. No matter what happens in our day-to-day life, there is always someone who cares, someone who asks little in return. Our dog provides us with a reason to rise in the morning, a reason to exercise, a reason to prepare food and, in some cases, a reason to live. We're never alone when we're in the company of a good friend.

*Labrador Retrievers can prove to be loyal hunting companions as well as household pets. Owners, Kathy and Ted McCue. Photo by Isabelle Francais.*

*You're never alone when you're in the company of a good friend! This is Brian Buffinton and his new Amberfield puppy.*

*Although your Labrador puppy may love to retrieve sticks, they can be dangerous. Instead, provide your pup with safe chew toys.*

# Preparing for Your New Puppy

This is a very exciting time for the whole family. A new member of your family will arrive shortly and there is a great deal of preparing to do.

The mother's instincts tell her to keep her puppies clean, warm, and

*Holidays are not the best time to bring your new Lab puppy home. There is usually a lot of commotion around the house during this time and the puppy may become scared or overexcited.*

nourished. In a few weeks this will be your job and you can start now by planning to buy the things your puppy will need to make his homecoming as comfortable and easy as possible.

Your puppy will need a place to call his own. The most effective way to create a safe and convenient place is to purchase a crate, which will also help you to housebreak your puppy quicker. Remember, dogs are den-dwelling animals and the need to feel secure is very important to them. A crate is a safe place for the puppy to be when you are out or

busy. The perfect way for you to introduce your puppy to the crate is to place a soft piece of indoor/ outdoor carpet about $1\frac{1}{2}$ feet deep into the crate and block off

*Remember that your puppy is leaving the company and warmth of his dam and littermates, so the first night may be lonely for your new family member. Here is a litter of chocolates and blacks from Amberfield Kennels.*

the rest of the crate with a piece of pegboard. The puppy only needs enough room to curl up and sleep and play with a few toys. *This crate is never used as a place of punishment.* Most medium-sized crates are approximately $2\frac{1}{2}$ feet wide by 3 feet high by $3\frac{1}{2}$ feet deep. Your dog will use this same crate when he is full grown. No matter how old your dog is, he will enjoy the security of his crate. The crate should be collapsible so you can move it to any room in the house.

You will want to be sure to feed the puppy the very best food available, so check with your breeder. Be sure to purchase puppy food, not adult formula food. Your breeder will be the best person to help you choose the brand that he has been using. Do not change the puppy's brand of food right away. This must be done gradually. Remember, buying in bulk is both convenient and economical.

Puppies need to be kept warm and away from drafts. Although they are adaptable to the weather, they will depend on you to watch out for them and to be aware of their needs, especially in inclement or very hot weather.

Water is an important part of

*When you bring your new puppy home from the breeder, do not change the brand of food right away. This must be done gradually. Photo by Isabelle Francais.*

your dog's diet. The thing you need to remember while housebreaking a puppy is that the water he drinks will eventually need to be eliminated, which means you will have to take him out to relieve himself. The amount of water he drinks will determine the number of times you will have to take him out. As your puppy grows, he will learn to control his intake of water to meet the schedule that you have set up for him.

This brings us to another important issue—your puppy's schedule. Following a schedule is not only the puppy's job but

*An Amberfield puppy bathing in the sun.*

the whole family's job. You must realize that your puppy is only a baby learning to be housebroken and his system relies on your punctuality and dedication.

Consistency is important even as your dog grows because the amount of food will increase as he grows older and it will take time for his body to adjust to this increase of food.

Toys are a must! The best way to encourage your pup not to chew your furniture is to supply him with chew toys and to never leave him unsupervised while out of his crate. Some toys are better suited for puppies than others, so be cautious when choosing a toy. Nylabones® are especially good because they won't upset the puppy's digestive system or

*Squeaky-toys can be fun but beware of the squeaker once the toy becomes ripped or torn—your puppy will eat anything. This tired little pup is owned by Mary Baker of Woodland Kennels in New York.*

*There is a plethora of wonderful chew items offered by Nylabone®
that can satisfy your dog's chewing needs from puppyhood to
adulthood. Photo by Karen Taylor.*

alter your housebreaking routine. Squeak-toys can be fun but beware of the squeaker once the toy becomes ripped or torn—your puppy will eat anything! There is a plethora of wonderful chew items offered by Nylabone® that can satisfy any puppy's need.

These few tips will help you enjoy your new family member and keep him safe as well. Love and praise your pup each and every day for blessing your family with his love and companionship.

*Remember that your Labrador puppy is really a baby and training requires lots of patience and understanding. Photo by Isabelle Francais.*

# Housebreaking Your Puppy

Every member of the family needs to realize that their most important job is to build consistency into the puppy's daily routine. The puppy will train easily if he knows what is expected of him; however, he can't do it alone. It is your and your family's job to stick to the schedule that is best for your puppy in order to ensure that he has a well-rounded lifestyle.

Training your puppy takes patience and understanding.

This puppy is really a baby and needs to be shown when and where he is allowed to go to relieve himself. Your first job is to designate an area of your yard that is suitable for your puppy to relieve himself. By suitable I mean an area off to the side of the yard that is easily accessible and easy to keep clean. Pick up your puppy and bring him over to this spot and allow him to smell around and become acquainted with the grass and the smells. The reason for establishing this area stems from the fact that dogs are traditionally den-dwelling animals and generally won't mess where they sleep. The kennel where your puppy came from may have used newspaper in an exercise pen and therefore your puppy may not be used to the grass and the outdoor smells. It might be helpful to bring some newspaper outside with you at first to help the puppy associate the purpose of bringing him to this special area.

The real routine begins at the next feeding. Since you have already prepared his crate with a piece of indoor/outdoor carpet, the puppy should be placed in his crate prior to mealtime. The proper amount of food should be allowed to

*Choose a spot in your yard that is suitable for your puppy to relieve himself and then allow him to sniff around and become acquainted with the grass and smells.*

soak in about one-half of an inch of warm water for about ten minutes before each meal, allowing the water to be absorbed into the food. This is important, especially in puppies under six months of age, to prevent bloating of the stomach. Since the crate is always representing a good, safe place for the puppy, his first meal should be served here. Place the bowl in the crate and close the door, permitting the puppy to eat undisturbed and undistracted. When he is done eating, offer him some clean cool water in his water bowl. Now it's

*Children should have an active part in the housebreaking process. This is Christle and her new Amberfield puppy.*

the house unless he has urinated and completely relieved himself of all his food.

In the beginning this may take some patience but it's best to establish this routine now while you have the time. Do not allow the puppy to develop bad habits, such as making you think he's done and then later eliminating in the house. Remember that whatever goes in must come out and it's best if you're the one in charge of where and when it does. This routine should be followed precisely after each meal in order to housebreak your puppy properly.

time to pick up your puppy and carry him out to his spot so he can relieve himself. *Important:* Don't take the puppy back into

There are other times when you must take your puppy out too! Most puppies are very active and inquisitive. You will notice that your puppy seems to like to sniff around the room, especially after a play session. It appears that he is just investigating; however, he is really sending you a message that he needs to go out to urinate.

You should be aware of this each

*You should always take your puppy outside upon waking up. This pup is owned by Julie Sturman of Ambleside.*

time your puppy wakes up or drinks water. Water is another important topic in housebreaking. During the initial stages of housebreaking, water should only be offered to the pup when you are willing to take him out immediately after he drinks it. The amount of water your puppy drinks throughout the day will determine the number of times he needs to be taken out. Also, no water should be given to the pup after about 7:30 in the evening. The idea is to empty the pup's system throughout the evening so he won't be able to wet in the crate in the middle of the night.

The routine of feeding the puppy in the cage is a good habit to develop in the beginning. As you will learn, puppies become very excited when they think they're going to eat and start jumping up to get at the bowl in your hands. This can start jumping, a bad habit that will be hard to correct and unpleasant, especially when you're dressed for work. Puppies will act like children, trying to get the best of you because they're so cute. After a while the cuteness wears off and big dogs that jump are very

*Time to go for a walk. Once your puppy becomes used to a schedule, he will let you know when he needs to be walked. Owner, R. Buffinton.*

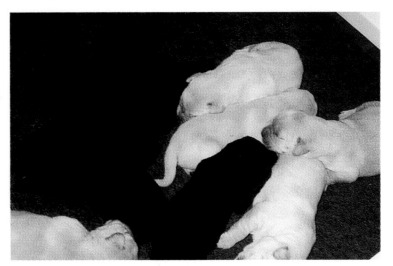

*Remember that your puppy just left a litter of brothers and sisters whom he would cuddle up with every night. It is only natural for him to be lonely at first.*

annoying.

The first few nights seem to be the hardest for you and the puppy. The evening feeding should not be any later than your dinner hour (preferably between 5:00 and 6:00 p.m.).

The puppy's system needs plenty of time to empty itself of all food before he is put in his cage for the night. For your convenience and the puppy's peace of mind, bring the cage into your bedroom and place it next to your bed so that he can see you. Remember that your puppy just left a litter of brothers and sisters whom he him train you! It's reasonable to assume that the first night he'll cry some before he settles down and will sleep for about a

*Four-week-old yellow Labrador owned by Woodland Kennels in New York.*

would cuddle up with every time he slept. It's only normal for him to be lonely at first. But don't let six- to seven-hour stretch. You might hear some whining or scratching, which means he might have to go out. After your trip outside, carry him back to the cage and say "good night" once again. Before you take him out in the morning, feed him in his cage (hint: let the food soak overnight so it's ready immediately in the morning and you just have to add a little warm water), then pick him up and carry him out to his spot. The reason for carrying him is to avoid any accidents on the way. Remember to be sure that he has relieved

*This eight-week-old black Lab pup is reaching an age where he will be able to control himself longer. Each day will bring new improvements.*

*Once your pup is fed and awake, he will want to play. Responsible owners make time for play sessions with their Labrador puppies.*

himself completely before going back into the house.

As the puppy grows, the need to be taken out in the middle of the night will stop. Usually the first three nights are the worst. As the puppy reaches nine weeks, his system is more developed and he can control himself longer. Each day will bring new improvements and more control. Never wake a sleeping puppy in the middle of the night.

*Ch. Amberfield's Beach Boy, owned by the authors, at seven weeks of age.*

Now your daily routine begins! Your pup will want to play. Now that he is fed and wide awake, be sure someone is able to spend some time with him while everyone is getting ready for the day. Bring the crate back into the family room or the kitchen during the daytime. Collapsible crates make this an easy task. It's most important to keep the puppy among the family and never shut away in a basement or bathroom.

There's nothing wrong with putting the pup back in the crate during breakfast if he seems to be begging at the table—this is one habit you don't want to encourage.

After a few more trips outside and a lengthy play session,

*Your puppy's day should consist of eating, playing and resting. This yellow puppy is owned by Bonnie and Ed Laub.*

the pup is ready for his morning nap back in his crate. This is your chance to do your errands, as he needs to rest for an hour or so. Lunchtime is around 11:30 or 12:00, especially when on a four-times-a-day feeding schedule for puppies from eight to 12 weeks. Once again, have food soaking so you can avoid any barking or crying when lunchtime arrives. Follow the same procedure of feeding him in the crate and then carrying him out to his spot. You'll be surprised how quickly he picks up the routine and looks forward to the consistency of your

*A wire pen like this one is the best kind of crate for your new Lab. Make sure it will be big enough for him to stand in when he is an adult.*

care. The rest of the day will be similar to the morning activities: eat, go out, play, rest, etc. The ideal time to spend quality "family time" with your puppy is when the family arrives home from school or work. Outside play or even just cuddling up together for some TLC is very important in strengthening the bond between you and your pup. Dinnertime will roll around again and everything is done the same as at lunch and breakfast.

Take your pup everywhere you go whenever possible (not so much to public places, though, until he's had all his shots, as many infections can be picked up from stray dogs). When traveling in the car, use his crate if your vehicle has the room. This way your puppy can travel safely and still be with you. Remember not to feed him just prior to traveling, as this can result in car sickness and ruin your pup's desire to travel. Always keep the car well ventilated on warm days and don't leave your dog unattended in a car for any long period of time.

*Cuddling up together for some TLC is very important in strengthening the bond between you and your pup.*

Following these tips might seem too rigid to you; however, your puppy eagerly awaits a schedule that he can depend on. The puppy's breeder took great care to ensure the pup's health and safety. It's your job to resume this responsibility and to enjoy the love your puppy has to offer.

*A black Labrador pup from Briar Run Kennels in New York.*

# Caring for Your Labrador Retriever

**FEEDING**

Feeding and exercising your puppy go hand in hand with the training or housebreaking schedule you establish.

The type of dog food you feed your puppy is usually best recommended by your breeder, as he will know which brand best

*Foundation bitch Agber's Darlyn from Amberfield Kennels and Andrew Livesey.*

*"Eat all your dinner, young man, and you'll grow up big and strong like me."*

facilitates the coat and condition of the dog. Labradors usually will do well on most high-quality dry kibble, which can be found in good pet-supply stores or a feed and grain store. It is also more economical to purchase a large quantity of food, such as a 40-pound bag, and keep it in a large plastic container, such as a new plastic garbage can with a tight lid to keep out moisture. Remember, human foods only cause weight gain, diarrhea, and bad habits. The number of feedings per day will decrease as the puppy becomes older. However, it is best to keep the feedings at twice a day with Labradors because they are generally very big eaters and will gorge themselves to death if given the opportunity. The best way to balance your dog's diet is to feed him twice a day, morning and evening, after six-months-old. There is only so much nutritional value that

*Labradors are generally big eaters and will gorge themselves to death if given the opportunity. These two pups owned by Frank Purdy are taking advantage of such an opportunity! Photo by Isabelle Francais.*

*Exercise for Labrador Retrievers is a must. Playing games with toys, such as products by Nylabone®, is a good way to ensure good, safe exercise with the added benefit of healthy teeth. Photo by Karen Taylor.*

can be absorbed out of one feeding. Therefore, two meals are better than one.

## EXERCISING

Exercise for a Labrador Retriever is a must; however, too much can cause problems with the dog's joints and hips. There have been many studies that show that hip dysplasia is 30 to 60 percent environmental. This means that overexerting the puppy at a young age can have damaging effects on the development of the hip sockets and the amount of calcification that occurs during early stages of the puppy's development.

Puppies should have a daily exercise routine. They will enjoy the consistency of knowing what to expect and will also look forward to the reward of playing and exercising with their owner. This type of moderate exercise is much safer than taking a long-distance jog with their master once a week. Puppies

*This Labrador Retriever is enjoying a game with his Gumadisc® by Nylabone®. Photo by Karen Taylor.*

should be taught to walk on a leash at around six months of age. Remember that you should be walking the dog—not him walking you. When walking only use a choke lead to keep the dog under control. The best way to maintain control is to make sure that the choke chain is properly sized for the

*Make sure that the choke chain is properly sized for your Lab. This is Marsh Dak's Shooting Star, CD owned by Dianne L. Schlemmer. Photo by Karen Taylor.*

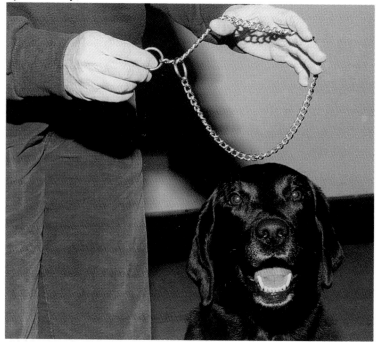

*Introduce your Labrador puppy to the water little by little.*

dog and that the chain is correctly placed under the dog's jaw and up behind his ears so very little tension is needed in order to keep the dog under control.

Labradors are water dogs. We know they originally swam in the frigid waters of Newfoundland and England. Teaching your Labrador puppy to swim can be exciting, but you need to introduce him to the water properly. A gently sloped incline is the best place to bring the puppy into the water because he can gradually walk in and swim. Your puppy's first experience will make a lasting impression. You'll find that most Labradors love to swim and will whine with anticipation each time you venture near their swimming hole.

The Labrador's versatility and sound disposition make him an easy pet to accommodate. He enjoys spending time outside in a kennel run as well as lying around the house. Of course, this depends on a positive introduction to the

*Ch. Amberfield's Beach Boy and Ch. Amberfield's Sugar Magnolia—inside or outside as long as we're together.*

*Labradors are water dogs. They love to swim and will whine with anticipation each time you venture near their swimming hole.*

outdoor kennel. Make sure the kennel run is safely designed, offering a dry shaded area that protects him from inclement weather. Dogs, by nature, are pacers. They require a sufficient amount of space to pace up and down. The width of the kennel is not as important—approximately 4 feet wide will suffice. The length should be from 14 to 18 feet. The surface should be covered by either a

*Provide your Lab with safe toys for him to chew on, especially during the teething period.*

cement slab or 3 to 4 inches of gravel. Dirt or grass areas can become muddy and may also fester parasites, which are detrimental to your dog's health. Be sure to provide sufficient toys and bones for your Lab to chew.

**GROOMING**

The Labrador's short dense coat is easy to care for. Regular brushing and an occasional bath to loosen the undercoat during shedding season is generally enough to maintain a good healthy coat.

There are a few different types of brushes that are very effective in helping to control the amount of shedding. The shedding blade, which is a flexible metal band with teeth that curves into a U-shape with two leather handles, gets out the undercoat. Most all dogs will shed in the spring so that they are more comfortable in the summer. A pin brush or a metal comb is all you need to use on a weekly basis.

Labradors don't usually have any smell to their coat; however, any extra time you spend on conditioning your Lab's coat will bring fine results. Most all Labradors will love the extra attention and you will find that you'll enjoy the time as well.

Many people believe

*Slicker brushes are especially helpful for removing mats from your dog's coat. Photo courtesy of Hagen.*

that an egg is good for a dog's coat. This is a myth. Only proper nutrition and vitamins will produce a healthy coat. There are many types of pet vitamins on the market so consult your breeder for advice. Liver treats are good for rewarding your dog (rather than using human food filled with fats and oils that make your dog overweight).

Caring for your dog's nails is very important! How would you like to walk on your toenails instead of the bottom of your feet? That's

*A grooming kit will provide you with the essential tools needed to properly groom your Labrador. Photo courtesy of Hagen.*

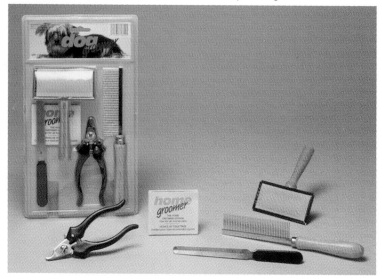

how your dog feels when his nails are too long. Nails that are clear in color are the easiest to clip because you can see the quick through the nail. Your breeder began clipping nails when the pup was only a few days old. You should continue to do so as needed throughout your dog's life. Routine clipping will prevent the quick from growing down too far into the nail. Further, the shape of the nail will usually become more pointed near the end and thicker at the base. The pointy part is the new growth and can be clipped off. This is very helpful on black nails because the quick is not visible.

*A healthy coat like the one on this yellow Lab owned by R. Buffinton is produced through proper nutrition and vitamins.*

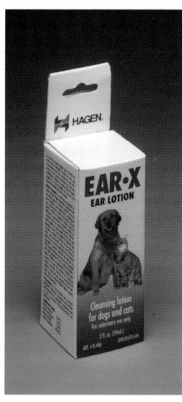

*There are special ear cleaners sold in pet shops that are very helpful in preventing infections. Consult your veterinarian. Photo courtesy of Hagen.*

Don't be too alarmed if the nail bleeds after clipping, just be sure to have a styptic stick on hand to stop the bleeding. Many dogs that walk on pavement don't need their nails clipped as often because the nails naturally grind down on the rough surface. As your dog grows, you will become accustomed to determining when you need to trim your dog's nails.

Labrador's ears require minimal care. The most important time is after swimming. You should wipe the ear canal and the flap dry; moisture can get trapped in these places and bacteria can cause an ear infection.

Use a cotton swab and only clean the area your hand can reach. There are special ear powders sold that are very helpful and can aid in preventing infections. Be sure to consult your veterinarian before administering any medication into your dog's ears.

Grooming will help strengthen the bond between you and your Lab. As you care for your pet, you'll notice many new personality traits and learn to reward him with the things he likes. Remember to keep a positive attitude and approach to grooming. Your dog can sense your anxieties and will respond much better to your confidence and reassurance.

*Labrador Retrievers have a soft, weather-resistant undercoat that provides protection from water, cold and all types of ground cover. Owner, Briar Run Kennels.*

*Due to their loving temperament and high intelligence, Labrador Retrievers are very easy to train. Owner, Amberfield Kennels.*

# Training Your Labrador Retriever

Instruction begins at home, the minute we introduce our pup to his new quarters. In the beginning, it seems as though every other word is "No," just as when we are running after a human toddler. But, eventually, we can attempt various other preschool lessons: "sit" for a treat, "lie down" while brushing, "stand" for pretty, "stay" for a split second, "outside" for potty, and so on. The dog's vocabulary will increase though yours seems to have regressed. Before you know it, you will need to expand his education and yours.

Most large communities have dog clubs or individuals that offer training classes. People who live in smaller towns or more rural areas may have to search a bit, but can often find trainers within a half-hour's drive. The time spent at classes is well worth the effort.

A good instructor has seen every problem in the book

and then some and can give you the benefit of his experience. Someone has always walked in your—and your

*Marsh Dak's Shooting Star, CD owned by Dianne L. Schlemmer participating in obedience class. Photo by Karen Taylor.*

dog's—footprints, no matter how annoying, embarrassing or frustrating.

Obedience schools usually require that a dog should be six months old or close to it. But there are other alternatives for early socializing and education. Puppy "kindergarten" is fun for everyone, dogs and people alike. Nothing is cuter than a pup, (except a bunch of pups) bouncing, bobbling and *boinnng*ing about. Even the most experienced owner is set back in finesse, while working with a wiggleworm, trying to avoid stepping on paws and encouraging acceptable puppy

*With the proper training, your Labrador can accompany you anywhere—even out on the open seas. This is Bonnie owned by Dr. and Mrs. Norman D. Phillips.*

manners. Lessons range from sit, stand and stay (for the vet) to nail clipping, basic grooming, walking on leash and coming on command. It's fun and amazing how quickly these youngsters grow, from the tiniest Chihuahua to a mighty Great Dane, and before anyone realizes, it's time to go on to a higher level of education.

Conformation classes often accept puppies as soon as their basic inoculation schedule is in effect, or at about eight weeks of age. Training for the breed ring consists of walking and trotting on leash.

The pup learns to stand and allow the "judge" to pet him all over, look in his mouth and examine his testicles. Tips to aspiring handlers are given as well, allowing us to get our feet wet before diving into the

*Through training, owners learn how to become and remain the leader in the twosome. Photo by Robert Smith.*

*In formal obedience classes, instructors inform owners about the proper kind of collar and leash to use. This is a well-behaved Amberfield's Darlyn watching the holiday parade.*

big pond of dog shows.

Class training, whether obedience, conformation or kindergarten, teaches the owners how to become and remain the leader in this twosome. Just like a good dance team, one leads and the other follows. Unless we want a dog who demands us to fetch and cater to his every whim, we'd better learn to lead.

Instructors inform enrollees about the type of leash and collar to use, but most suggest a chain link or "slip" collar, with a

*Amberfield's Catch Me Kate is ready to help water the flowers.*

leather leash. Probably 90 percent of the class simply wants a pet who doesn't jump up on everybody who comes to the door or can walk to the corner without tripping his owner. Class instruction includes basic obedience routines, however, so that the person who wishes to show his dog can do so competitively.

Obedience exercises include heeling (on and off leash), standing, sitting, staying, lying down and coming when called. All of us can take advantage of those handy commands even if we

*A well-trained Labrador can learn almost anything!
Owner, Elaine Perkins.*

never set foot in a ring.

How nice it is to tell a dog "Down" just as he jumps up to greet us with muddy paws or to say "Stand, stay" so that the veterinarian can examine him.

*Ch. Agber's Darlyn, by Summer Sun II ex Agber's Dandilion.*

# Prevention and Cure— A Healthy Life

Every owner hopes that his dog will live a long healthy life. Nowadays, this desire is enhanced through careful selection of puppies and breeding animals, modern technology and veterinary care and the family's care and concern—all of which aid in prevention and cure.

Dogs today are so much more fortunate than their ancestors. Regulations which were originally passed to protect property, livestock and humans actually ensure a dog's safety as well.

Licenses and the accompanying taxes provide shelters for lost or abandoned animals, and a tag may prove to be a lifeline to home. Because leashes and confinement are now required by law, fewer families allow Rover to rove, and have his life ended by a bullet or highway traffic.

Many diseases commonly fatal in the early to mid-1900s are now prevented through inoculation. An old-time exhibitor understood that if he took his dog to enough shows, the animal

*Before you bring your new Lab puppy home, he should have already received one full set of inoculations.*

would contract distemper sooner or later. It was common to lose entire litters to the dreaded disease, which plagued canines for hundreds of years. Now, thanks to a nearly universal vaccination, most breeders have never even seen a case.

As recently as 1978, parvovirus swept the canine world, decimating kennels. As with all diseases, it was the very young and the very elderly dogs that succumbed in great numbers. Thanks to modern research laboratories and the pharmaceutical companies, within two years a preventative vaccine was available.

## GENERAL MEDICAL CARE

Before a puppy is sold, he should have received at least one full set of inoculations, protecting him from distemper, hepatitis (adenovirus), leptospirosis, parainfluenza and parvo. Many breeders vaccinate against corona virus and bordatella as well. Among the puppy's stack of official papers

*A real family picture. Front: Jenny and Mindy; back: Sam, Maggy, Rambo, Abby, and Bitty. Owners, Mr. and Mrs. Snow.*

*With proper preventive care, your Labrador pup will be able to grow with the family. This is Paul Sousa and his puppy from Breezy Labradors.*

that are turned over to the expectant parents should be a list noting the ages when additional shots will be needed. Although the schedule varies from breeder to breeder, or one veterinarian to another, the following is an example: six weeks—combination DA2PP & Cv; nine weeks—parvo; twelve weeks—combination; sixteen weeks—parvo and rabies.

Before the puppy goes to his new home, he should be examined by a veterinarian and pronounced healthy and free of major congenital defects. Most bite, eyelid, testiculate, cardial and esophagael problems can be detected before eight weeks, as can luxated patellas and open fontanels. From that point on, it's up to the new owners to continue examinations and veterinary care to keep him healthy. Routine health care, of course, includes yearly vaccinations and heartworm checks, followed by administration of the preventative.

## PARASITES

Taking stool samples to the vet should be part of the annual examination or when observing symptoms such as diarrhea, bloody stools or worm segments. Dogs,

*A healthy yellow Labrador puppy owned by R. Buffinton.*

especially puppies, may vomit and lose weight when infested with parasites. Hookworms, roundworms, tapeworms, whipworms, coccidia and giardia are common. They can be eradicated with the proper medication but could be dangerous if left untreated. An over-the-counter drug may not be the right one for the particular parasite which your dog is harboring.

## FLEAS

Bugs bug us and our pets. Fleas cause itching and carry tapeworm eggs. The resultant scratching can irritate the skin so that rashes and hot spots develop. Dogs lose hair, scratch and chew at themselves and are miserable. In attempting to exterminate the pests, owners tear their hair, scratch their heads, chew their nails and are also miserable. Better to prevent than to cure, but for everyone's sanity, once the invasion has occurred, the sooner the evacuation, the better.

Talk to your veterinarian about the proper products to use, then arrange a regular reconnaissance to prevent a losing battle with fleas. During the warm months of the year, many people spray or powder

*Puppies can easily pick up parasites from contaminated soil. Regular worming of your dog along with proper hygiene can help alleviate this problem.*

*If your dog has fleas, washing him with a flea shampoo will help to eradicate them. Photo courtesy of Hagen.*

the slightest scratch, they look for telltale evidence—skittering teeny bugs or flea dirt, which looks like a sprinkling of pepper. It's usually easiest to see the freeloaders on the less hairy groin, belly or just above the root of the tail.

Among the products used to combat flea pests are dips, collars, powders, sprays, tags and internals—drops or pills. Instructions should be followed implicitly not only for best results, but because some of these products contain ingredients which may cause problems themselves if used carelessly.

animals (including other pets who may pass fleas to your dogs) once a week and premises (house and lawn) once a month. In between, owners keep up flea surveillance. At

If the critters are found, shampoo or dip

all dogs (cats, too, with a product labeled safe for them), and spray living and sleeping quarters. It doesn't do any good to treat the animal without debugging the environment or vice-versa. One flea who escapes will happily reinfest all over again. If the infestation is heavy, it may be necessary to fog your house and to repeat the procedure a few weeks later. All animals must be removed from the premises for the period of time specified on the fogger can.

*Make sure your dog is treated with a flea powder or spray during the warmer months when fleas are at their worst. This is Ch. Killingworth Bonny of Dimeno, CD, CGC in her garden. Owner, Ambleside Kennels.*

In addition to the regular regime, many owners spray before walking dogs in areas where they are likely to pick them up, e.g., woods, pastures, training and show grounds. Most flea pesticides also kill ticks, and daily grooming sessions should include running your fingers through the dog's coat to find engorged ticks. Natural, non-insecticidal products can safely be used on a daily basis in the on-going war on fleas.

## LYME DISEASE

One species of tick, *Ixodes scapularis*, the tiny deer tick, is the prime culprit which transmits the germ that causes Lyme disease to humans and animals. Deer ticks are found on mammals and birds, as well as in grasses, trees and shrubs. They are rarely visible because they are so

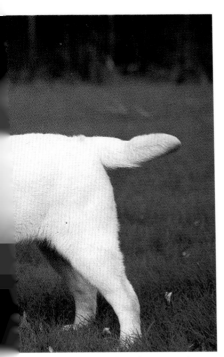

*After your dog has been outdoors examine him for fleas and ticks.*

small (as minute as the dot above an i), but the damage they can cause is magnified many times their size.

Lyme disease can damage the joints, kidneys, heart, brain and immune system in canines and humans. Symptoms can include a rash, fever, lameness, fatigue, nausea, aching body and personality change among others. Left untreated, the disease can lead to arthritis, deafness, blindness, miscarriages and birth defects, heart disease and paralysis. It may prove to be fatal.

People should cover

themselves with protective clothing while outdoors to prevent bites. Repellents are helpful for both dogs and humans. Examine the body after excursions and see a doctor if symptoms appear.

*First aid cream for dogs is available at pet shops. Photo courtesy of Hagen.*

## SKIN DISORDERS

Dogs, just like people, can suffer from allergies. While people most often have respiratory symptoms, dogs usually exhibit their allergies through itching, scratching, chewing or licking their irritated skin. These irritations often lead to angry, weeping hot spots.

Allergies are easy to detect but difficult to treat. Medications and topical substances can be useful, in addition to avoidance of the irritant, if possible.

## CERF/OFA/VWD CERTIFICATION

Good breeders want to produce healthy, sound animals. The best way to do this is

*Breeders want to produce healthy, sound Labradors. Photo by Robert Smith.*

to start with healthy, normal animals judged to be free of hereditary conditions which can cause lameness, blindness and other disorders.

In the early years of dog shows, when symptoms of disease appeared, owners asked the opinion of experienced local breeders and veterinarians. As time went on, more specifics were learned about these various diseases and their heritability. Veterinarians took x-rays, performed blood tests and diagnosed symptoms. Now we are fortunate to have experts in various areas. Due to their specialized training and the numbers of cases these experts see, they are more likely to be accurate. Some have formed organizations which register clear animals and certify dogs free of hereditary disease.

Probably the first organization of its type, the Orthopedic Foundation for Animals (OFA) certifies dogs free of hip dysplasia upon clearance of an x-ray by three board-

*Chocolate Labrador Retriever owned by Denise Evans. Photo by Isabelle Francais.*

*In order to produce healthy, sound animals a breeder must begin with animals that are judged to be free of hereditary conditions. This is Agber's Darlyn, a foundation bitch from Amberfield Kennels.*

certified radiologists. Dogs must be two years old for lifetime certification. The OFA also reads and gives opinions of radiographs with evidence of other heritable bone disorders such as craniomandibular osteopathy (CMO), osteochondritis dessicans (OCD), ununited anchoneal process, Legg-Perthes disease and fragmented chronoid process. The organization's address is OFA, 2300 Nifong Blvd., Columbia, MO 65201.

Eye problems can be

detected by veterinary opthalmologists available at teaching hospitals, private specialty practices (in larger cities) and at eye-screening clinics hosted by kennel clubs. These specialists examine for cataracts, entropion, pannus, retinal dysplasia, luxated lens, progressive retinal atrophy (PRA), central progressive retinal atrophy, Collie eye anomaly and other hereditary eye conditions. The Canine Eye Registration Foundation (CERF) may be contacted at CERF Veterinary Medicine Data Program, South Campus Courts, Bldg. C., Purdue University, West Lafayette, IN 47907. The age of the dog at first testing depends a great deal on the breed and the specific area of concern. A few diseases are apparent in puppyhood. CERF requires an annual examination for certification of freedom from some diseases.

Von Willebrand's disease (VWD) is a bleeding disorder, similar to hemophilia. Clinical signs include lameness, aching joints, bloody stools, chronic bloody ear infections or a failure of the blood to clot. A blood test measures for adequate concentration of a specific clotting factor.

*Before you breed, make sure that your dog is free from hereditary diseases. Although this may involve some cost, it is not as expensive as attempting to replace faulty pups.*

Although it may be conducted in puppies as young as seven weeks, it should not be done within one month of vaccination; therefore, most are five or six months old. If a dog is in heat, has just whelped a litter or has been on antibiotics, the test should also be postponed for one month. Other disorders that are limited to just one or two breeds also have specific tests. Blood samples can be sent by your veterinarian to Dr. Jean Dodds, Veterinary Hematology

Laboratory, Wadsworth Center for Laboratories and Research, NY State Dept. of Health, PO Box 509, Albany, NY 12201-0509.

Before you breed, determine whether or not your dog is free of these and other hereditary diseases. Although the tests involve some cost, they are not as expensive as attempting to replace faulty pups. And they are certainly much less costly than a broken heart or a damaged reputation.

## BONE DISEASE

Many canine bone diseases have gained nicknames—albeit not affectionate—due to the unwieldy medical terminology. For

*Ch. Polywog Comic of Chidley, owned by Amberfield Kennels.*

instance, canine cervical vertebral malformation/ malarticulation syndrome is referred to as "wobbler" syndrome; panosteitis is shortened to pano; and canine hip dysplasia is often simply called CHD. The first symptom is usually a limp. Diagnosis is made through a radiograph of the affected area.

Craniomandibular osteopathy (CMO) affects the growth of bone in the lower jaw, causing severe pain. Spondylosis is the technical name for spinal arthritis.

Hip dysplasia is a poor fit of the hip joint

*Always keep your Lab's eyes clean and free from foreign matter. This is Ch. Amberfield's Beach Boy, owned by the authors.*

into the socket, which causes erosion. Wobbler syndrome affects the neck vertebrae, causing weakness in the hindquarters and eventually the forequarters. Osteochondrosis dissecans (OCD) affects joints, most often the shoulder, elbow or stifle. Ununited anchoneal process, commonly referred to as elbow dysplasia, is a failure of the growth line to close, thereby creating a loose piece in the joint. Kneecaps which pop out of the proper position are diagnosed as luxating patellas. Legg-Perthes, most often seen in small breeds, is a collapsing of the hip joint. They all result in the same thing: pain, lameness and, left untreated, arthritis.

The exception is pano, which is a temporary affliction causing discomfort during youth. Pano may be visible on x-rays, showing up as a cloudiness in the bone marrow in the long bones, particularly in fast-growing breeds.

**EYES**

Entropion is a condition in which the eyelid rolls inward. Eyelashes rub and irritate the cornea. In ectropion, the lower eyelid sags outward, allowing dirt to catch in the exposed sensitive area and irritate the eye. In addition, extra

*Jake and Moony taking a rest. Owner, Tammy Ader.*

eyelashes grow inside the lid which rub the surface of the eye and cause tearing. Either can be treated topically or, if severe, surgically.

## ORGANIC DISEASE

Heart disease affects canines as much as it does humans. A dog suffering from a problem involving the heart may exhibit weakness, fainting, difficulty breathing, a persistent cough, loss of appetite, abdominal swelling due to fluid retention, exhaustion following normal exercise, or even heart failure and sudden death. Upon examination, an abnormal heart rhythm or sound or electrical potential might be detected, or changes in speed or strength noticed.

Treatment includes first stabilizing any underlying condition, followed by medications, low-sodium diet, exercise restriction and, possibly, surgery.

Chronic renal disease may first show up in vague symptoms—lethargy, diarrhea, anemia, weight loss and lack of appetite—as well as increased thirst and urination. Kidney disease is more common among geriatric canines. It may be compensated to some extent through diet. Diagnosis is most often made through blood and urine tests.

## GASTRIC TORSION

Because a dog's stomach hangs like a hammock, the ends are effectively shut off if it flips over. Nothing can enter or exit. The normal bacterial activity in the stomach causes gas to build with no release through vomiting or defecating. The gas expands and, just like a balloon filled with helium, the stomach bulges and bloats.

It's physical torture for the dog and mental anguish for the owner who sees his dog moaning in agony and retching in a futile attempt to relieve the pressure.

*Frequent exercise and plenty of fresh air are essential to your Labrador's good health. Photo by Robert Smith.*

With the veins and arteries to the stomach and spleen also closed off, shock sets in which can be rapidly fatal. Torsion—medically termed

*Ch. Amberfield's Bo Regard owned by Marci and Dave O'Brien.*

breeds, know there is no time to waste whether it's the middle of the night, a holiday or vacation time. It is urgent to reach a veterinarian who can treat the shock, followed by surgery to reposition the twisted organs. During surgery, the veterinarian may tack the stomach to the abdominal wall to prevent recurrence.

## AUTO-IMMUNE DISEASES

Auto-immune disease, like cancer, is an umbrella term that includes many diseases of similar origin but showing different symptoms. Literally, the body's immune system views

gastric dilatation and volvulus (GDV)—is an emergency. Experienced owners, particularly of large

*Three happy, healthy Labs from Amberfield Kennels enjoying some playtime together.*

one of its own organs or tissues as foreign and launches an attack on it. Symptoms depend on which system is the target.

For instance, hypothyroidism symptoms can include lethargy, musty odor, temperament change, decreased fertility or unexplained weight gain, in addition to the more suggestive thin dry hair, scaliness of the skin, and thickness and darkening of the skin. Testing for hypothyroidism (which can be from causes other than auto-immune disease) may be conducted as early as eight to twelve months, using the complete blood count, blood chemistry, thyroid T4, T3 and free T4 tests.

Rheumatoid arthritis is a result of an auto-immune reaction to the joint surfaces. The resulting inflammation and swelling causes painful deformed joints. If the red blood cells are perceived as foreign invaders and destroyed, the rapid onset anemia (called auto-immune hemolytic anemia) can cause collapse and death if diagnosis and treatment are not

*A healthy active Lab competing in an agility trial. Photo by Karen Taylor.*

quickly initiated. Often an auto-immune reaction in an organ causes destruction of that organ with subsequent loss of function. Auto-immune disease of the adrenal gland leads to hypoadrenocortissism (Addison's disease).

The same reaction in the thyroid gland soon has the dog exhibiting symptoms of hypothyroidism. Auto-immune diseases of the skin are called pemphigus, while those of connective tissue are termed lupus. Many other varieties exist, and each requires specialized testing and biopsy. Most respond to treatment once a diagnosis is made.

## EPILEPSY

Probably because of the feeling of helplessness, one of the most frightening situations a dog owner can face is watching a beloved dog suffer seizures. As in people, epilepsy is a neurological condition which may be controlled by anticonvulsant drugs. Many breeds of dogs have a hereditary form of epilepsy usually with an adult onset.

The University of Pennsylvania Canine Epilepsy Service has conducted studies of drugs and dosages, their efficacy and long-term side effects, to assist veterinarians in prescribing anticonvulsants.

## ALTERNATIVE TECHNIQUES

During the 1970s and 80s, acupuncture, chiropractic and holistic medicine became part of the canine health picture. Veterinarians who have received special training in these fields now practice their techniques on patients who do not respond to or cannot take previously prescribed medical treatments. Patients have responded favorably to these methods, especially when done in conjunction with medical supervision. Certainly, when it comes to a much-loved animal, the most recent up-to-date techniques should be tried before resorting to euthanasia. Owners should be aware, however, that practitioners must have a veterinary degree to chiropractic and acupunctural treatment should not take the place of standard veterinary

*Epilepsy is a condition that is hereditary. Only dogs that are known to be free of this condition should be bred. Photograph courtesy Keith Thompson.*

practice on animals and that the holistic, medicine, but instead should enhance it.

## GERIATRICS

As dogs age, problems are more likely to occur, just as they do in their human counterparts. It is even more important to examine your dogs, noting every "normal" lump and sag, so that if a new one occurs you are aware. Owners should make appointments for veterinary check-ups at least once a year.

Elderly canines suffer the same infirmities as we do when we age. Deafness, arthritis, cancers, organ disease and loss of

*"Doc said I should cut down on the cigars!" Owner, Woodland Kennels.*

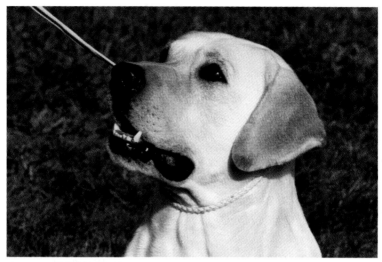

*Your Labrador's life can be extended through precautions and routine veterinary care.*

vision are common. Symptoms such as a cough, bloating, weight loss, increased water consumption and a dry thin coat are warning signs to seek medical attention. Many aging patients can be made comfortable and sustain a quality life.

Although our dogs will never live long enough to satisfy us, we can extend their lives through our precautions, specialized nutrition, exercise and routine veterinary care.

## EMERGENCIES

The get-your-vet-on-the-phone-drive-there-as-quickly-as-is-safe emergency situations are few, thankfully. But they do occur, and that's why all owners should be aware of symptoms. Veterinarian numbers for day and night calls should be posted prominently near the phone.

Occasions that are well worth a middle-of-the-night payment are: shock, anoxia (choking), dystocia (labor and whelping complications), hemorrhage, gastric torsion, electric shock, large wounds, compound fractures and heat stroke. In addition, neurological symptoms such as paralysis, convulsions and unconsciousness indicate an emergency. If your dog has ingested poison, been severely burned or hit by a car, for instance, call an emergency number for help.

## EUTHANASIA

Most owners dread facing the decision of euthanizing a pet. But as hard as it is to make that decision and drive a beloved animal on his final journey, it is more difficult to watch a dog who has lost all quality of life struggle through a day-to-day fog of pain. Of course, it's also more

*Responsible owners afford their Labradors the best possible quality of life. This is Ch. Maestros Song, WC owned by Gordon W. Sousa, Jr.*

stressful for the animal, and don't we love him enough to spare him that trauma? Certainly, eyes that plead "Help me" deserve a humane response.

Euthanasia is a fact that most breeders

and pet owners must eventually face if they do not wish their animals to suffer. Ask your veterinarian to administer a non-lethal anesthetic or tranquilizer, literally putting the dog to sleep while you hold your pet and caress him gently. The dog will drift off to sleep peacefully and without fear, no longer suffering. At that point, the veterinarian injects a lethal overdose of anesthesia which instantly stops the heart. Death truly comes as a servant in peace; euthanasia is a kind, quiet death.

Arrangements should be made for the disposition of the body prior to the euthanasia. Some owners wish to bury the remains themselves (be aware of local regulations,

*Ch. Killingworth Bonny of Dimeno, CD, CGC babysitting her Cavalier King Charles Spaniel friends. Owner, Ambleside Kennels.*

however, which are becoming more stringent) or to have the dog cremated. Others want the veterinarian to handle the arrangements. Planning ahead saves more difficult decisions during the trauma of losing your friend.

## VETERINARY SPECIALISTS

With a surplus of small animal veterinarians expected in the latter part of the 20th century, and a surging volume of knowledge and medical technology, many veterinary school graduates elect to specialize with additional courses and training. These include surgery, dentistry, oncology, radiology, neurology, cardiology, dermatology, ophthalmology, theriogenology (reproduction) and internal medicine.

This "overpopulation," naturally, is a boon to pet lovers. If your dog has one of these problems, your veterinarian may refer you to a board-certified specialist or contact one for advice on specialized treatment. Any concerned, caring veterinarian will be happy to do so and assist his patient to live a healthier, fuller life.

Everyone who owns dogs for very long begins to build a canine medical chest. Basic supplies should include cotton, gauze, tweezer, ipecac, muzzle, styptic powder, cotton swabs, rectal thermometer, petroleum jelly, hydrogen peroxide, ear medication, anti-diarrhea preparation, ibuprofin painkillers and one-inch adhesive tape. Include first aid instructions and a poison help sheet with a hotline number.

## ETHICS

In all diseases, symptoms may vary from mild to severe.

In the most extreme cases, victims may have to be euthanized. Many do live, however, under veterinary care and supervision, occasional medication and owner TLC. Nevertheless, it's important to know which diseases are known to be inherited. Our dogs can carry the factors which transmit hereditary conditions and pass on their afflictions to a higher than normal percentage of their progeny. Affected dogs should be spayed or neutered and never allowed to transmit their discomfort to future generations. Owners

Veterinary medicine has come a long way in helping our dogs to live longer and fuller lives.

should also be aware that AKC regulations specify that surgically corrected dogs may not compete in the breed ring.

# Emergency First Aid for Your Lab

## PULSE

Pulse determines the speed, the rhythm, and the strength of a heartbeat. It gives you clues to the physical condition of the animal. Pulse increases with fever, hemorrhaging, paralysis, and disease. It also increases with exercise, excitement, fear, hot weather, severe pain, and eating.

The normal pulse range for dogs is 70 to 120 beats per minute. The older and larger a dog is, the slower his pulse will be.

## HOW TO TAKE A PULSE

1. All of the arteries (blood vessels that lead away from the heart) have a pulse.

2. The most common artery used to find a pulse is the femoral artery because it is large and easy to find. It runs down the inner surface of the hind leg.

3. The best place to take the pulse is up by the groin area on the inside of the back leg.

4. With the dog standing, place hand on artery.

*A dog's pulse increases with exercise. Photo by Robert Smith.*

5. Gently roll artery under fingers until you find a good pulse. Do not use your thumb.

6. Count pulse beats for 30 seconds and double that to figure out the number of beats per minute.

7. This should be done when your dog is at rest and again after he has engaged in some hard exercise so that you have the normal range for your

dog. Knowing his pulse will be helpful when trying to determine if he is ill.

## THE NATURE OF FEVER

It is easy to tell when a dog is sick, but not so easy to tell what is wrong. It is difficult because many diseases have the same symptoms. Common symptoms for many illnesses are: fever, loss of appetite, lack of energy.

Fever is one of the earliest signs that something is wrong. Be sure to know the difference between a rise in temperature and a fever. Normal dog temperature is 101 to 102 degrees. A dog's temperature will rise following exposure to heat or exercise, since they cannot perspire as humans do to rid themselves of extra heat.

The symptoms of a fever are:

1. Abnormal rise in temperature
2. Loss of appetite
3. Hot, dry skin
4. Increased thirst
5. Rapid heartbeat and/or heavy breathing.

Be sure and take a reading at least twice a day when monitoring a fever.

## HOW TO TAKE A TEMPERATURE

1. Shake mercury down in bulb.
2. Lubricate bulb.
3. Gently glide

*Knowing first aid for dogs can make a big difference when faced with an emergency. Yellow Lab puppy photographed by Robert Smith.*

thermometer into dog's rectum, holding it in place if needed.

4. Hold in standing position with other hand under stomach if necessary.

5. Read after three minutes.

After following the steps of taking your dog's pulse and checking for fever symptoms, you now have enough information to determine whether your dog needs immediate assistance. This vital information will be helpful to your vet in determining the extent of the emergency.

*Ch. Amberfield's Beach Boy and handler Joy Quallenberg.*

# So You Want to Show Your Lab

## RULES OF THE GAME

Showing your dog can be fun and rewarding as well as the most frustrating experience you have ever encountered.

Your dog must meet certain requirements to compete in AKC-licensed dog shows. Your dog must be registered with the AKC in order for you to obtain an AKC registration number. A blue registration

*Although dog shows are exciting, they are a lot of work for both handler and dog.*

slip should have been obtained when you purchased your Labrador Retriever. After the form is completed, it is sent to the AKC with a fee to apply for registration. Among other items, you will need to decide upon a proper name for your dog. If you purchased your animal from a breeder, they may require their kennel name on the certificate or may have already selected a show name for your dog. This name is for your dog alone and may not be duplicated to another dog or changed.

Other requirements for showing include a minimum age of six

*Labrador Retrievers can be shown in all three colors: black, yellow and chocolate.*

months, an animal that is neither deaf or blind, and an animal who is unneutered.

## GETTING YOUR FEET WET

Before jumping into dog showing, whether on your own whim or someone else's, I strongly recommend that you attend several local shows in your area and simply observe. You will see many strange sights. Much of what you see will probably make little or no sense at all.

Realize that dog shows came about as a way to evaluate breeding stock. There are people who have been breeding dogs for more than 20 years and approach showing dogs very differently from the single owner and dog combination, which is becoming more common over time. Take the time to know who the important people are in your breed. If you're lucky enough to become acquainted with established people within your

*This is Deborah Sousa with Ch. Talwoods Abigail, CD, WC, an all-around Labrador Retriever. She got her championship, her obedience degree and her working title all in the same year.*

breed, learn from them and all of their experiences.

If you have acquired a "show-quality"

puppy and want to show him, I recommend taking the puppy for an evaluation by a knowledgeable person within your breed. You may have to bring your dog to a show for a breeder or handler to look at. Be prepared to hear an honest evaluation, even if your opinion differs from theirs.

**GETTING THE GO AHEAD**

Your dog is now registered and has been approved by several experienced people...now what?

I recommend showing a puppy eight to ten times within a short time frame (one to two months) in order to acquaint the animal with the show ring. During this time, the emphasis should be on fun and positive experiences, not strict training. I have seen many owners show puppies that have been so over-trained that they are bored and unresponsive in

*Bring your Lab to dog shows to acclimate him to strange noises and strange people.*

*Ch. Amberfield's Sugar Magnolia's first stack at eight weeks old.*
*Basically, a puppy should be taught to stand still for an examination.*

the show ring. So, how much is too much?

This depends a lot on the animal's personality and your level of ability. Basically, a puppy should be taught to stand still for an examination. The dog must allow the stranger to examine his teeth, body structure, etc., in order to complete the evaluation of your dog. A puppy should also be leash trained and know his name. He should also be socially aware and unafraid of strange noises, people, and situations. So, what's so difficult about that?

This is where you must decide to what degree you want to show your dog and what your goals are.

## CAN I DO IT?

The art of handling show dogs is a natural ability for some and a painstaking learning experience for others. You must look at yourself objectively and decide if you are able to train and show your dog successfully in the show ring. To discover your hidden talents and start your dog's training, I recommend attending a show-handling class.

*Ch. Amberfield's Beach Boy came from the first home-bred litter at Amberfield Kennels and finished his championship at 15 months with five majors and two Bests of Breed from the classes.*

These are held by local dog clubs. Some classes are better than others; however, a novice will benefit from any class. The basics, including stacking and gaiting, should be taught in any class. Any class will also start training your dog to become socially aware. Information about local breed clubs can be obtained from the AKC, located in New York City, New York.

For those of you who admit that you can't show your own dog, there are other options, such as professional dog handlers who abound in the dog game. These are dedicated individuals who have made showing dogs their life's work. If you have attended several shows, you will notice an agent's name next to an animal's name in the show catalog. Many of these people are professional handlers.

## SO YOU WANT TO HIRE A PRO

Approaching a professional handler is not hard, but getting their attention may be. Keep in mind that they are working at a show and may not be available to speak to you. However, once you do get a chance to speak to one, discuss your plans for your dog openly. A true professional will need to evaluate your dog for show potential. If he feels your animal is worthy, obtain a rate card and show schedule. Listen to the professional about the best way to prepare your animal

*Ch. Briary Brendan of Rainell, en route to the title, going Winners Dog at Westchester Kennel Club in 1976. Owned by Lorraine and Barbara Getter.*

and yourself for the experience. Please do not faint upon reading the rate card. Hiring a professional handler is expensive. Usually entry fees, road expense fees, and board fees are additional to the handler's fee per show.

If you are serious about all of this, it would be wise to allow the handler to keep your dog for a period of time before showing

*Ch. Sandyland's Rip Van Winkle, owned by Gordon Sousa.*

*This is Ch. Amberfield's Surfer Girl winning Best of Breed.*

him. The animal and the handler need some time to get to know each other. If you are going to spend a small fortune on having your dog shown, you should try to attain the highest level of success in doing so.

This includes, but is not limited to, a period of adjustment for your dog to adapt to all the changes that are about to occur in his daily life.

## GOING TO CAMP

Whenever a new dog comes to my facility and leaves his owner for the first time, I refer to it as "sending a child to camp." First, be certain that the handler has adequate facilities to keep and condition

*Professional handler Joy Quallenberg and an Amberfield Lab having some fun before the show work begins.*

must realize that sending your dog away from home is going to be traumatic for both of you. There are several things you can do to prepare for the transition.

One of the most important things is to accustom your dog to a crate. An animal who is with a handler will spend many hours in a crate both at a show and while being transported to and from a show. If an animal is not accustomed to confinement and is having a difficult time adjusting to kennel life, he may begin to stress out. Stress can show itself in many forms, including aggression,

your animal. Make sure they are secure, clean, and odor-free.

You, as the owner,

submission, not eating, attempting to escape, etc. It is imperative that an attempt be made by the owner to help the animal become accustomed to as many stress-producing factors as possible.

Another area many people neglect is grooming. Just because he is a Labrador does not mean he should not be groomed. Table training an animal and getting him used

*If you plan on showing your Lab, one of the most important things you must do is accustom him to being confined. Photo by Isabelle Francais.*

to having his ears and teeth cleaned and nails trimmed will help eliminate more stress factors

*Professional handlers often handle more than one dog at a time. This is Joy Quallenberg showing a handsome black male.*

that your dog may encounter with a handler.

Please make sure that your animal is clear of all external and internal parasites and that he is up to date on all shots. I recommend obtaining an inoculation to help prevent an occurrence of kennel cough.

If your animal is properly conditioned, trained, and socially adjusted, you should expect to see results within ten shows with the handler. There are no promises; however, you should have a successful experience showing your dog. Good luck and happy showing.

*Don't worry about leaving your dog in the hands of a professional handler. Handlers form special bonds with each of their charges. This is Joy Quallenberg with Mellow.*

*Conformation shows are the most numerous of the competitive events.
This is Joy Quallenberg with Ch. Amberfield's Beach Boy.*

# The Dog Show Sport

The AKC was founded in Philadelphia, Pennsylvania on September 17, 1884 by 12 dedicated sportsmen interested in establishing a uniform set of rules for the holding of dog shows. From then on, the Board of Directors has been made up of dedicated amateur sportsmen.

Each year, more than 8,000 competitive events are held under AKC rules. These are mainly dog shows, field trials, and obedience trials. For all of these, there are licensed events, point shows where championship points or credit towards field and obedience titles may be earned and informal events, like match shows where no points or credits are earned.

## CONFORMATION SHOWING

Dog shows are the most numerous of the competitive events. The emphasis here is on conformation. Judges examine the dogs and place them according to how close (in their opinion) they measure up to the ideal called for in the official standard.

There are two types of conformation licensed dog shows: specialty and all-breed shows. Specialty shows are limited to dogs of a specific breed or group of breeds. All-breed shows are for all AKC registered dogs. The first AKC dog show was held in Mineola, New York on October 7, 1874. It included classes for Pointers, Irish Setters, Gordon Setters, and "Setters of Any Breed." In order to understand the growth of the sport today, keep in mind that there are over 1000 all-

*Specialty shows are limited to a particular breed or group. This is Scrimshaw Call Mee Madame at the Labrador Specialty of Potomac in Leesburg, Virginia.*

*Handlers come in all sizes. This is Agber's Darlyn and Seth Livesey.*

breed shows held annually.

Judging is the process of elimination that ultimately results in one dog being selected as Best in Show.

### What's The Point?

Most dogs at conformation shows are competing for points towards their championships. To become an official AKC Champion of Record, a dog must earn 15 points. These points are based upon the number of dogs actually judged within your breed on that day. The number of dogs needed for various amounts of points varies from area to area and also by sex in order to equalize competition nationally. In other words, it would be easier to win points in Puerto Rico than in New York, since there would be fewer dogs competing in Puerto Rico than in New York on an annual basis.

A dog can earn from one to five points at any show. Wins of three, four, or five points are considered Majors. To earn a championship your dog must win two such Majors under two different judges. This can be done in several ways. At a dog show there are six regular

classes in which dogs needing points may compete: puppy, 12 to 18 months, novice, bred-by-exhibitor, American-bred, and open.

The judging is the same for every breed. Puppy classes are

Ch. Amberfield's Beach Boy, Ch. Aurums Aladdin and Ch. Amberfield's Good Vibration in the stud dog class on the Cherry Blossom Circuit in Leesburg, Virginia.

fourth. The first place winner of each class stays for further competition. The judge then judges the 12 to 18 class, novice, bred–by-exhibitor, American-bred, and open classes repeating the procedure used in the puppy class. When he finishes all of the classes, the winners are called back in to compete against each other. This is called the Winners Dog class. The judge then repeats the procedure but only selects one winner and that dog receives the number of points to be awarded for the day. This procedure is then repeated with all the bitch classes. (Yes, dog shows are a sexist sport!)

always first. In each class the dogs are evaluated and the best four are placed first, second, third, and

*At conformation shows, judges examine dogs and place them according to how close they measure up to the standard. This is Scrimshaw Call Mee Madame.*

After the Winners Bitch has been selected the Champions on Record and the unconfirmed champions enter the ring for the Best of Breed judging. An owner may enter his dog as a champion for 30 days after the animal has met all necessary requirements for his AKC title without official notification of champion status. The judge selects one dog as Best of Breed for the day. Then between the Winners Dog and Winners Bitch they select a Best of Winners. If either the Winners Dog or Winners Bitch are selected Best of Breed then they are automatically Best of Winners. The judge then ends the breed judging by selecting a Best of Opposite Sex to Best of Breed.

This takes place for all the breeds at a show. Then each breed winner competes in his

*Ch. Lockerbie Stanwood Granada, owned by Mrs. Helen Warwick, Lockerbie Labradors.*

respective Group. Four placements are awarded in each Group and the winner of each Group goes on to Best in Show competition where only one dog will remain victorious.

## OBEDIENCE

Many owners sign up for a training class, hoping the results will give them a well-behaved pet. At discovering the yet untapped intelligence of our dogs, we yearn to find out just how good they really are.

For many owners, the goal is to gain titles (Companion Dog, CD; Companion Dog Excellent, CDX; Utility Dog, UD; Utility Dog Excellent, UDX) which proclaim their pets'

ability and their own prowess in training. Three passes (or legs) under three judges,

*Marsh Dak's Shooting Star, CD clearing the bar jump in obedience. Owner, Dianne L. Schlemmer. Photo by Karen Taylor.*

and that's enough.

But a few hone the competitive edge, going for an Obedience Trial Championship (OTCh), as well as top wins in individual breeds and in all-breeds. To win an OTCh, the dog must garner 100 points from winning first or second placings in Open and Utility Classes against all breeds, including those who already have their OTCh. Capturing High in Trial (HIT), whether at an all-breed, specialty or national show, is a coup that all serious competitors seek.

Special trials such as the Windsor Classic, the Gaines Regionals and Classic—which is considered the Super

Bowl of the obedience world—attract the best working teams in the country. Amazing precision does not remove the obvious pleasure of the dog to be working with his best friend.

All of this brings the bonus of a good companion, one with enough manners to keep his nose out of the guests' cocktail glasses and who waits politely for his own potato chip without too much drooling or too many mournful looks.

## TRACKING

When it comes to tracking, our dogs always beat us by a nose. Canines have 40 times more olfactory sensory cells than humans do, and that's why they have such busy noses. Why not put to good use all that business of tracing down every crumb on the floor and sniffing at each other and visitors in embarrassing places?

Tracking, unlike the other obedience titles, can be earned at any time, before the CD, after the UDX or anywhere in between.

A dog's been using his nose since birth when he followed it to his mother's table setting. Allowing the dog to do what comes naturally is not always easy for owners, however, because we're used to running the show. Training to track often consists of teaching the handler to "lay off" and to take directions from the dog, as well creature comforts. Tracks are laid in the rain, the cold and the heat, as well as on

*When it comes to tracking, our dogs always beat us by a nose. Owner, Lori A. Brittle. Photo by Isabelle Francais.*

as steering the dog's nose in the right direction and on command.

The second hardest thing about tracking is forgetting about beautiful, balmy days. They're laid in muck and frost and amongst ragweed tickling our noses, as well as in lovely, grassy pastures; over

*This yellow Labrador pup is exercising his tracking abilities. Owner, Frank Purdy. Photo by Isabelle Francais.*

hill and dale in addition to flat surfaces. You get the picture—training must also be performed under such conditions so that the dog tracks during any trick of Mother Nature. Not only that, early morning is the best time to train while the dew is still on the roses. . . and the ground.

If you and your dog hold up to snuff and enjoy the great outdoors, then there's the TDX (Tracking Dog Excellent).

## HERDING AND FIELD TRIALS

Each of these have stylized the trials for the type of dog, i.e., spaniel vs. pointer vs. retriever; shepherd vs. collie vs. cattle dog. In other words, a German Shorthaired Pointer is not expected to do field work like a Golden Retriever or an English Springer Spaniel. A Shetland Sheepdog works a flock differently than a German Shepherd or a Corgi does.

If you like the combination of dogs and horses and you

*Field trials involve the dog's working relationship with man. Photo by Robert Smith.*

*For a Lab, return of the game must be prompt and tender. Photo by Robert Smith.*

wing and to the noise of guns.

Dogs work two at a time, in a brace, for up to an hour with handlers and judges following on horseback. When a point is made, the handler flushes the birds, the official gunners shoot the bird and the dog is sent to retrieve. Wins are judged on verve, style and stamina as well as manners. Field trials are also held on foot after rabbits for Beagles, Bassets and Dachshunds. Sharp working dogs may attain a Field Trial Championship.

Herding trials follow an obedience format, with three passes to attain a title, three

have a Beagle, Basset Hound, Dachshund or sporting dog, then field trials might be your bag. Locating and pointing hidden game birds are the object of this sport. Dogs (and handlers) must be steady to the sudden flushing of birds to titles and a Championship title: Herding Started (HS), Herding Intermediate (HI), Herding Excellent (HX) and Herding Champion (HCh).

Cattle, sheep, goats or ducks may be used as stock in course A (for driving and farm/ranch dogs such as Australian Cattle Dogs, Bouviers, Corgis, Smooth Collies and Old English Sheepdogs). Sheep or ducks may be used in course B (fetching, gathering type dogs, such as Border Collies, Rough Collies, Beardies and Shelties). Sheep are used in course C for boundary herding dogs

*Sportsmen that participate in field trials learn proper training and the expansive abilities of their dogs. Photo by Robert Smith.*

such as Pulik, Briards, German Shepherds and the Belgian herders. Each course has specific requirements. A Malinois who works like a Bouvier is not required to enter course C; however, he may be entered in course A.

*Through field trials, the intelligence of such trained dogs is demonstrated. Photo by Robert Smith.*

## CANINE CITIZENSHIP

In an effort to promote responsible dog ownership and good canine members of society, the AKC approved the Canine Good Citizen Tests in 1989. We have long since passed the time when dogs were allowed to roam at will—creating destruction, havoc and more puppies or alternatively being fed by the butcher, the baker and the candlemaker with benign good will. Today's dog must learn to adapt to modern, crowded society.

Dogs perform the tests on leash and are graded either pass or fail. The evaluators consider the following:

1. Does this dog's

behavior make him the kind of dog which they would like to own?

2. Would this dog be safe with children?

3. Would this dog be welcome as their neighbor?

4. Does this dog make his owner happy—without making others unhappy?

There are ten tests. The dog must:

1. Be clean, groomed, healthy, and allow touching and brushing by the evaluator.

2. Accept a stranger's approach.

3. Walk on a loose lead under control—as though out on a walk.

4. Walk through a crowd.

5. Sit for an exam while a stranger pets him.

*Today's dog must learn to adapt to modern, crowded society. Mellow and Darlyn are well-behaved canine citizens.*

*The Labrador Retriever is regarded as the foremost retriever of upland game birds. Photo by Robert Smith.*

6. Sit and down on command.

7. Stay in position. Additionally, the entry is judged on its reaction to:

8. Another dog.

9. Distractions such as loud noises, sudden appearance of a person or a person with an object such as a bicycle.

10. Being left alone for five minutes.

**INSTINCT TESTING**

During the 1980s, the American Kennel Club encouraged getting back to the basics training with instinct tests. Their hunting tests began in

1985 and have been enormously successful, growing faster than anyone expected.

In 1990, AKC approved herding tests as a sanctioned sport. National clubs encourage natural instincts by sponsoring water tests for Newfs, tunnel tests for terriers, lure coursing for sighthounds, coaching trials for Dalmatians, weight pulling and carting for working dogs, and sledding for nordic breeds. The only test for toy breeds at present is a daily one for all dogs—companions for their owners.

All of these instinct tests are pass or fail. Either the dog does it

*Unlike so many other breeds, the Labrador, whether working or show dog, has strong intact instincts for retrieving. Photo by Robert Smith.*

. . . or he doesn't. This format is great for the pet owner who simply wants to see if his dog can do more than be pretty. Yes, he can work like he was meant to.

*Few breeds of dog (and most ducks) can boast the possession of webbed feet. The Labrador's webbed feet make swimming an easy feat. Photo by Robert Smith.*

can do what he was supposed to do 100 or more years ago when the breed was first developed. The tests are also a way for the show exhibitor to prove that, yes, his dog

Hunting tests are divided into Junior, Senior and Master stakes with different formats for retrievers, pointing dogs and flushing spaniels. Basic herding test

*A Labrador Retriever in optimum shape is able to work a whole day on the field retrieving on land and in water. Photo by Robert Smith.*

classes are divided into Preliminary and Principal. When the dog has passed both, he receives an HT (Herding Tested). The more complicated Pretrial Test shows more advanced training and a passing dog receives a PT (Pretrial Tested).

When a dog has never before been trained or exposed to his erstwhile duties, it's amazing and exciting for owners to watch a dog "turn on." As the dog's attention is caught, his posture changes to one of alertness. Eyes become intense and muscles twitch in readiness.

These tests are also good news for the person who is non-competitive or has limited time or budget to spend on doggy activities. Further information on these events may be obtained from the American Kennel Club, Performance Events Dept., 51 Madison Avenue, New York, NY 10010, and through books written on these particular subjects.

Yes, a dog can be attractive and conform to the standard and can still work. Maybe next, truffle hunting trials for Poodles.

### AGILITY

Agility is almost more fun than work, and it's certainly fun for those watching it. Although a few people are beginning to take it seriously, most entries simply want to see if their dog can and will conquer the obstacles.

Originating in the United Kingdom in 1977, agility has begun popping up at more and more American shows as well. The

*Labrador Retriever clearing the bar jump at an agility trial. Photo by Karen Taylor.*

object is for the dog to take on each obstacle as quickly as possible and without making a mistake. These include jumps, a scaling wall, a rigid tunnel, a collapsible tunnel, a hoop, seesaw, wall, water jump and almost any other barrier a club can invent. There are also a table and a pause box, where the dog must stand on top for five seconds.

The best time and performance wins. Relay teams increase the challenge and fun. Clubs may offer courses for large dogs and for small dogs. Agility is held as a non-regular obedience class under AKC rules.

*The Seeing Eye in Morristown, NJ flies in dog guides from all over the country to aid people in need.*

# The Labrador as a Guide Dog

There are many organizations all over the world that supply guide dogs to visually impaired people. Having been a breeder for over 15 years, I've never felt as close to the breed as I did when I visited The Seeing Eye in Morristown, New Jersey.

I know the breed well; however, I guess I never really understood its potential. Now I look upon my own dogs with more affection and respect than I ever thought possible. I learned about the work of The Seeing Eye and the "very special role" the guide dog plays in a blind person's life. A Labrador's versatility, adaptability, and keen sense of dedication to people's needs make him ideal for assisting people as a guide dog. We readily accept guide dogs because we have come to understand how important they are in helping blind people to become independent and lead normal lives. However, years ago this philosophy was not so widely accepted.

The story of the guide dog's beginnings is remarkable and heartwarming.

The Seeing Eye was founded in 1929 by an extraordinary woman, Dorothy Harrison Eustis. She was a German Shepherd breeder, originally from Philadelphia, who lived for many years in Switzerland. Dorothy Eustis was determined to prove to the world the idea that a dog could give blind people their freedom of mobility and a "richer life." She trained the first guide dog, a German Shepherd named Buddy, for a young man named Morris Frank. Through his desire to help other blind people to become independent, Morris Frank, along with Buddy, struggled to prove that there was a need for guide dogs and that they should be allowed in

*The Seeing Eye spends weeks training the companion as well as the guide dog to work together as one and build trust in the guide dog's judgment.*

restaurants, on public transportation, and in all public accommodations.

Since 1929, The Seeing Eye has placed over 10,000 highly trained guide dogs with qualified blind people. In 1979 the school began using Labradors. Today an equal amount of Labradors and German Shepherds are trained for the program.

According to Douglas Roberts, Director of Programs and 25-year veteran of training guide dogs, "a sound temperament and initiative" are two key characteristics that make a Labrador an ideal guide dog.

Walt Sutton, a Seeing Eye dog trainer

*Trainers have dedicated themselves to training the perfect guide dogs. Photo courtesy of The Seeing Eye.*

*The Labrador's versatility, adaptability and keen sense of dedication to people's needs make him an ideal guide dog.*

breeding, soundness and a stable personality have been consistently reproduced in The Seeing Eye Labs. Guide dogs must be able to work in any situation, whether it be a city street, subway, or even an elevator. Very often a guide dog is required to sit quietly under a desk in an office all day. This is not difficult for a Labrador. Mr. Sutton says, "Labradors are well suited and versatile for people of all ages. They are easygoing and flexible, as well as accommodating in virtually all situations."

A guide dog must have steady nerves and must always be alert when responding to

says, "Labradors always obey their masters. They are always willing to please rather than trying to outsmart their masters." Through years of careful either his trainer's or his companion's commands. For instance, if a blind person misjudges the noises of oncoming traffic or if a car runs a red light, according to Mr. Sutton, "the dog kicks in and becomes your backup generator; it's the dog's responsibility. Whatever your dog does, you have to follow, because at that point he's the only one that really knows what's going on."

Whenever a guide dog disobeys his command because of

*Guide dogs are companions for life. Photo courtesy of The Seeing Eye.*

potential danger to his companion, it is considered "intelligent disobedience." A guide dog's stamina and endurance are vitally important, as he is trusted to guide under any condition.

The size of the dog and the amount of grooming the dog requires are important aspects to consider when choosing a guide dog. Many people travel; therefore, the dog has to be able to fit in airplanes and buses. When choosing a guide dog, the blind person has to make sure he is able to groom his dog properly. Remember,

*Family and training are important factors in developing well-rounded guide dogs.*

when out of harness, guide dogs are like any other lovable pet—ready to be a member of the family.

Labradors thrive on affection; therefore, they adjust to any response or tone used when completing a job merely by the words "good dog." Most guide dogs don't usually need a heavy reprimand, the correction can be made through repetition of the correct maneuver and a verbal response of "Phui!", which means "shame on you." All dogs have specific instincts that develop as they mature. For this reason, a guide dog must be trained not to react to these instincts,

*At The Seeing Eye, breeding has been perfected to meet the needs of an even temperament and well-rounded disposition.*

such as chasing a cat or digging a hole after a small rodent. A guide dog is the eyes for a blind person and cannot afford to falter at any time because it could endanger his companion. Verbal commands are the way in which the blind person communicates with the guide dog. The commands are "forward," "right," and "left." Guide dogs must be ready to respond at any given moment.

We are all very fortunate to have access to guide dogs. One never knows if or when one might need to depend on these loyal and intelligent animals. The Seeing Eye and the various other schools that train guide dogs have given blind people the opportunity to pursue life with greater independence, dignity, and self-confidence.

*A cute puppy from The Seeing Eye in Morristown, NJ.*

*A puppy trainer is an important part of the puppy's development as a guide dog. Photo courtesy of The Seeing Eye.*

*One of the roles of the Labrador Retriever as a detector dog is searching suitcases for drugs. Photo by Isabelle Francais.*

# Labradors as Detector Dogs

When you gaze upon your Labrador curled up on the kid's bed in the morning, it's hard to imagine him sniffing out an explosive, walking on suitcases searching for drugs, or scanning through rubble from a fallen building. These are some of the roles the Labrador plays as a detector dog. The pure nature of the Labrador Retriever enables him to be trained to perform most any task with determination and perfection.

The process of training a detector dog is very specific and should only be attempted by someone who has worked with specialists in the field. The expression "detector dog" means that the dog has been trained to identify a particular odor or scent. Detector dogs must have quality characteristics; this means they should have a solid disposition, a high retrieving drive, sound health, and a good association with the work.

Labrador Retrievers are not aggressive by nature. When a young child takes a squeaky toy right out of your dog's mouth, with half an arm still down his

Buster is part of the Bergen County Canine Unit in New Jersey. He is trained to detect the odors that possibly started this fire.

throat, you know your Lab has met the qualifications we're talking about. People tend to feel the need to associate with detector dogs as part of the community, as they do with their friendly policemen.

The Bergen County Police of New Jersey have been using detector dogs in their programs since 1974. Chief of Police Joel Trella says, "The Labrador has the ability to use his nose, the stamina to work long and hard, and the willingness to please the handler and still maintains a good attitude, which makes the dog superb as a detector dog." Chief Trella explained

*Detective Bob DiPalma and Buster on an arson job. Photo courtesy of Bergen County Canine Unit.*

that there is a place for both aggressive and passive dogs in detector work. For instance, arson and drug dogs can have an aggressive attitude toward their work because that will help them to complete the job of locating the source of the odor. A bomb detector dog, on the other hand, should have a passive personality considering the nature of the job. There are a significant number of Labrador Retrievers who can do the work required of detector dogs. The police are as equally concerned with the selection process of detector dogs as you are with the selection of your pet. They too are aware of the possibilities of getting a dog with a flaw that could interfere with the dog's work. Therefore they go to a reputable breeder who will help them locate a quality animal.

The police are able to utilize the temperament of the Labrador. For instance, Labradors thrive on retrieving games and each time a dog is let out of his kennel he looks for the reward of playing and retrieving. "They are able to narrow the dog's focus to a singular activity,"

says Chief Trella. They can actually test dogs by offering them some roast beef or a retrieve toy. Properly motivated detector dogs will choose the retrieve toy over the roast beef. The police are always careful not to jeopardize the dog's safety. There have been instances when an area was covered with hazardous chemicals and the policemen were able to protect themselves with proper protective clothing; however, the dog was not. It's in situations like these that the dog is not expected to complete a search.

Detector dogs build close relationships with their handlers. It

*Detector dogs build close relationships with their handlers. Photo courtesy of Bergen County Canine Unit.*

takes years for a man to trust his dog totally. But in time their relationship builds and the man learns to respect the true nature of his dog, which makes it possible for him to trust the dog. Sometimes human beings make mistakes because they allow other distractions to interfere with their decisions, but dogs usually don't because they are guided solely by their instincts. When a dog doesn't work to the handler's satisfaction, he has to ask himself—what did *I* do wrong? It is the handler's responsibility to direct the dog properly.

Chief Trella says, "Anyone can be a successful dog handler if he has patience, has the willingness to take direction, is introspective, and works to understand the true nature of the dog." Many times people say he'll do it for me. Does the dog really do "it" for you or for himself? Breeders and dog handlers agree that the best trained Labradors do "it" for themselves. It's the nature of the Labrador to be happiest when he is working. Consistency is the key to training a dog; even if you are consistently doing something wrong, you are probably better off than not being consistent at all.

Like guide dogs,

*Buster inspecting the remains of a burned building. Photo courtesy of Bergen County Canine Unit.*

detector dogs display "intelligent disobedience." There are times when an officer gives his dog a command and the dog doesn't respond for some reason unknown to the officer at that moment. However, moments later the dog has saved the officer's life by "intelligent disobedience."

To illustrate, Chief Trella and his detector dog had been in search of three male suspects for hours. They were doing a field search through a wooded area near a suburban housing track and were just about to wrap it up when the dog went on an off-lead search. This dog was a very experienced dog who was about eight years old. Chief Trella called his dog to come and the dog disobeyed his command. He called him again and this time the dog looked at the three-foot fence, looked at him, and looked back and forth several times between the two. The dog indicated a cigarette pack on the ground near the fence and sure enough the suspects had gone over the fence. Chief Trella gave his dog a stroke and then gave him the command to find the men. The dog then barked at the garden shed where the men were hiding. In this case Chief Trella trusted his dog's disobedience, which resulted in the apprehension of the suspects.

# Canine Companions for Independence

Visiting the Canine Companions for Independence training center is quite an experience. If you're fortunate enough to be free of any handicaps, you will marvel at the strength and determination that disabled people possess as well as the intrinsic depths of a dog's ability to help his master.

The simplest task of picking up a pencil, opening the refrigerator, or turning on a light switch is second nature for most people. For someone with a physical disability, these tasks can be simply impossible.

When someone calls our name, the fire alarm sounds, or the telephone rings, we usually respond without even thinking. For someone with a hearing disability, locating the sound or even knowing a signal has sounded is impossible.

Canine Companions for Independence is an organization that provides dogs as companions to disabled people. This service was founded by Bonnie Bergin, in 1975, with the help of a black Labrador Retriever named Abdul. Abdul became the companion of a quadriplegic woman and ever since that day the dream of helping others through the companionship of a dog became a reality. Now, Canine Companions for Independence has reached out to all parts of the United States through their five training centers which are located in: Santa Rosa, California; Rancho Santa Fe, California; Orlando, Florida; Farmingdale, New York; and Eden Prairie, Minnesota.

There are three types of assistance dogs: service, hearing, and social. Service dogs help people who have physical disabilities do everyday activities and lead a life of independence. Hearing dogs alert the person to sounds that they can't hear or locate the direction of the sound. Social dogs help people socialize and interact, such as children with developmental disorders or elderly people with other handicaps.

Labrador Retrievers play an intricate part in the CCI program. Over the years, 45 to 50 percent of all service dogs used by CCI have been

Labradors because of their personality traits, fine intelligence, and physical strength. Service dogs learn approximately 90 commands by the end of their two-month training session. Many of these commands may be given by voice alone, as some companions may have limited use of their arms and hands. These dogs also can become the arms and legs for many people who are confined to wheelchairs. Service dogs are trained to make transactions in grocery stores by placing items on the counter and giving the cashier the money. Service dogs often retrieve articles, such as keys, pencils, and even clothing. Some people have even trained their dog to help them get dressed. As a service dog, a Labrador has the strength to pull his companion's wheelchair when he becomes tired, as well as the intelligence to learn numerous commands.

One of the most remarkable things I have seen is a Labrador named Kosmic help his companion Travis, a nine-year-old boy, stand up. Travis has a muscle disorder that prevents him from bending his legs and ankles. Kosmic has learned to help Travis stand up by lying on the floor and allowing Travis to roll onto his back. As Kosmic gently stands up, so does Travis.

These companion dogs perform many tasks that we take for granted, like carrying books to school or the library, getting items off the shelf in a store, taking packages out of refrigerators, and even putting clothing in the washer. The solid and sound temperament of Labradors makes them very desirable for this unique kind of job. The companion must be a dog who can focus on people, who is compliant, who has the energy to perform some strenuous tasks, and who is secure in his environment.

CCI has developed their own breeding program because they require their dogs to be in the best physical health and to have a good disposition. With the help of foster families, CCI sends puppies out at about eight weeks of age to be housebroken and socialized. Most puppy raisers have their puppy for about 15 months and then send them back to the training center for specialized training. Trainers from CCI work consistently for eight months training the dogs and teaching them commands. Paul Mundell, Director of the Farmingdale Training Center in New York, mentions that "trainers are teaching the dogs the basic building blocks, which when put together, will meet the individual needs of each person." He stresses that a service dog's training is fairly complex.

Students who qualify for a canine companion go to the center every day for two weeks to learn how to work with their dog. Those who successfully complete the training graduate with their canine companion. Puppy raisers and family members of the graduates attend the graduation ceremony. This graduation is very emotional for all those involved in training and raising the CCI dog, as well as for the graduates and their families. For some CCI graduates, having a canine companion means the ability to live without a full-time attendant for the first time. For others, it is a chance to regain independence lost through illness or accident.

CCI's motto is "Exceptional Dogs for Exceptional People." Canine Companions for Independence is a non-profit organization and very often volunteers are used to help exercise the dogs at the training centers, so even you can become involved!

# Service Dog Organizations

People who wish to find help or make a donation to a service organization can contact the following:

## GUIDE DOGS

**Eye of the Pacific and Mobility Services, Inc.**
2723 Woodlawn Drive
Honolulu, HI 96822

**Fidelco Guide Dog Foundation**
P.O. Box 142
Bloomfield, CT 06002
203-243-5200

**Guide Dog Foundation for the Blind, Inc.**
371 E. Jericho Turnpike
Smithtown, NY 11787
516-265-2121

**Guide Dogs for the Blind, Inc.**
P.O. Box 1220
San Rafael, CA 94915-1200
415-499-4000

**Guide Dogs of the Desert**
P.O. Box 1692
Palm Springs, CA 92262
619-329-6257;
619-329-1287

**Guiding Eyes for the Blind, Inc.**
611 Granite Springs Road
Yorktown Heights, NY 10598
914-245-4024

**International Guiding Eyes, Inc.**
13445 Glenoaks

Boulevard
Sylmar, CA 91342
818-362-5834

**Leader Dogs for the Blind**
1039 S. Rochester Road
Rochester, MI 48063-4887
313-651-9011

**Leader Dog Project**
Michigan Department of Corrections
Huron Valley Women's Facility
5311 Bemis Road
Ypsilanti, MI 48197
313-434-6300

**Pilot Dogs, Inc.**
625 West Town Street
Columbus, OH 43215
614-221-6367

**The Seeing Eye, Inc.**
Box 375
Morristown, NJ 07960
201-539-4425

# DEFENSE DOGS

**Department of Defense Dog Center Headquarters**
Air Logistic Center (AFLC)
San Antonio, TX 78236-5000
1-800-531-1066

**National War Dogs Memorial Project**
President Joseph J. White
P.O. Box 6907
Jacksonville, FL 32236
904-693-3539

# SEARCH AND RESCUE

**American Rescue Dog Association**
P.O. Box 151
Chester, NY 10918

**Air Force Rescue Coordination Center**
HQ, ARRS/AFRCC
Scott Air Force Base, IL 62225-5009

**National Association for Search and Rescue**
P.O. Box 3709
Fairfax, VA 22038

HEARING DOGS
**Canine Companions for Independence**
P.O. Box 446
Santa Rosa, CA 95402-0446
707-528-0830 (V/TDD)
**Canine Working Companions, Inc.**
RD 2, Box 170
Waterville, NY 13480
315-861-5215 (TDD)
**Connecticut K-9 Hearing Dog Training**
239 Maple Hill Avenue
Newington, CT 06111
203-666-4646
203-666-4648 (TTY)
**Dogs for the Deaf**
10175 Wheeler Road
Central Point, OR 97502
503-826-9220
**Ears for the Deaf, Inc.**
1235 100th Street S.E.
Byron Center, MI 49315
616-698-0688 (V/TDD)
**Hearing Dog Program of Minnesota**
3865 Minnehaha Avenue South
Minneapolis, MN 55406
612-729-5986
**Hearing Dogs, Inc.**
290 Hamilton Road North
Gahanna, OH 43230
614-763-4282
614-471-7397 (TTY)
**International Hearing Dog, Inc.**
5901 E. 89th Avenue
Henderson, CO 80640
303-287-3277

**Iowa Hearing Dog Program, Inc.**

2258 Logan Avenue
Waterloo, IA 50703
319-236-2987
(V/TDD)

**New England Assistance Dog Service**

P.O. Box 213
West Boyleston, MA 01583
508-835-3304

**PawsAbilities**

Community Medical Center
2827 Fort Missoula Road
Misoula, MT 59801
406-728-4100

**Paws to Listen, Inc.**

P.O. Box 855
South Bend, IN 46624-0855
219-287-4273

**Phydeaux's for Freedom, Inc.**

1 Main Street
Laurel, MD 20707
301-498-6779

**Red Acre Hearing Dog Farm**

P.O. Box 278
Stowe, MA 01775
508-897-8343
(V/TTY)
508-897-5370

**Responsible Pet Ownership**

**Canine Health Mates**

3624 Fisher Road
Palm Harbor, FL 34683
813-787-5433

**San Francisco SPCA Hearing Dog Program**

2500 16th Street
San Francisco, CA 94103
415-554-3020

**Southeastern Assistance Dogs. The Speech, Hearing and Learning Center, Inc.**

811 Pendleton Street
9-11 Medical Court
Greenville, SC 29601
803-235-9689

803-235-6065 (TTD)

**Southeastern Hearing Ear Dog Program**
Baptist Hospital
Box 111
2000 Church Street
Nashville, TX 37236
615-329-7807
615-329-7809
1-800-545-HEAR

**Wisconsin Academy for Graduate Service Dogs**
Rt. 1, Box 139
Janesville, WI 53546
608-752-3990

SUPPORT DOGS

**Aid Dogs for the Handicapped**
1312 Bergan Road
Oreland, PA 19075
215-233-2722

**Canine Companions for Independence**
P.O. Box 446
Santa Rosa, CA 95402-0446
707-528-0830 (V/TDD)

**Canine Working Companions**
RD 2, Box 170
Waterville, NY 13480
315-861-5215 (TDD)

**Dogs for Independence**
P.O. Box 965
Ellensburg, WA 98926
509-925-4535

**Freedom Service Dogs, Inc.**
980 Everett Street
Lakewood, CO 80215
303-234-9512

**The Companion Dog Connection, Inc.**
3865 Minnehaha Avenue South
Minneapolis, MN 55406
612-729-5986

**Helping Paws of Minnesota, Inc.**
P.O. Box 12532
New Brighton, MN 55112
612-924-2404

**New England
Assistance Dog Service**
P.O. Box 213
West Boyleston, MA
01583
508-835-3304

**Paws With a Cause**
1235 100th Street S.E.
Byron Center, MI
49315
616-698-0688
(V/TDD)

**Phydeaux's for
Freedom, Inc.**
1 Main Street
Laurel, MD 20707
301-498-6779

**Responsible Pet
Ownership**
3624 Fisher Road
Palm Harbor, FL
34683
813-787-5433

**Southeastern
Assistance Dogs
The Speech, Hearing
and Learning Center,
Inc.**
811 Pendleton Street
9-11 Medical Court

Greenville, SC 29601
803-235-9689
803-235-6065 (TTD)

**Support Dogs for the
Handicapped, Inc.**
P.O. Box 966
St. Louis, MO 63044
314-487-2004
314-739-3317

**Wisconsin Academy for
Graduate Service Dogs**
Rt. 1, Box 139
Janesville, WI 53546
608-752-3990

THERAPY DOGS
**Center for Pet Therapy**
336 E. 71st St., #9
New York, NY 10021
212-535-3917

**Paws Across Texas**
7037 Culver Avenue
Fort Worth, TX 76116
817-732-3092

**Wisconsin Academy for
Graduate Service Dogs**
Rt. 1, Box 139
Janesville, WI 53546
608-752-3990

# INDEX

# New from T.F.H.

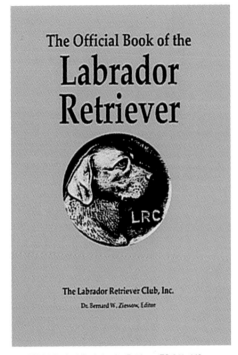

The Official Book of the Labrador Retriever TS-241, 448 pp.

Authored and endorsed by The Labrador Retriever Club, Inc., *The Official Book of the Labrador Retriever* is an entire library of excellent information in one timeless book illustrated with hundreds of beautiful photographs of the most important Labrador Retrievers of all time.

# More Labrador Books from T.F.H.

PS-905 352 pp.

*The Labrador Retriever* is a "must" for anyone involved in the breed—whether at a professional level or as an experienced owner. The comprehensive text is enhanced by the inclusion of hundreds of illustrations (many of significant historic value) as well as 43 full-color photos.

H-1059 480 pp.

*The Book of the Labrador Retriever* is a most ambitious work about the breed. Labrador history and husbandry are covered in exacting detail, highlighted by beautiful photographic coverage (with many photos in full color) of Labradors and Labrador owners of today and yesterday.

# All-Breed Books from T.F.H. Publications, Inc.

KW-227, 96 pp.
100 color photos.

SK-044, 64 pp.
Over 50 color photos.

TW-113, 256 pp.
200 color photos.

H-1061, 608 pp.
100 B&W photos.

TS-101, 192 pp.
Over 100 photos.

H-1016, 224 pp.
135 photos.

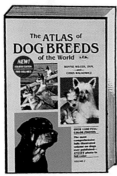

H-1091, 2 Vols., 912 pp.
Over 1100 color photos.

TS-175, 896 pp.
Over 1300 color photos.

TS-220, 64 pp.

TS-205, 156 pp.
Over 130 color photos.

H-1106, 544 pp.
Over 400 color photos.

TS-212, 256 pp.
Over 140 color photos.

TS-220, 64 pp.